Never Too Late

A West African Woman's Saga
A Journey of Captivity, Perseverance,
Faith and Liberation

by Patience (Aisien) Karsten

ISBN: 9781648589102
Copyright © 2020 by Patience Karsten

Never Too Late
by Patience (Aisien) Karsten
missionarymedics1@gmail.com
www.MissionaryMedics.org

Design of *Never Too Late* book cover and contents by Inspired Graphics, LLC, Copyright © 2020 Inspired Graphics, LLC
Lynn Hitchcock, Designer
www.InspiredGraphics.org
lynnh@inspiredgraphics.org

Introduction

Life throws a lot at us—challenges here and there—and sometimes it seems the whole world is against us. At that point, even the air we breathe seems to hurt. However it goes, keep your faith strong and never give up for it is never too late!

To all who have this book in their possession, even after my demise, I hope this finds you well. My message to you with this book is to endure and forgive. I am not trying to hurt my children, family, friends, or anyone. I just have to tell the true story of my life and get it off my chest. Many people hurt me and I forgive them all. If you read my story and you find yourself in the same situation or close, never give up! The future is bright, but you must forgive. I love you all! Love covers a multitude of sins. ~ *Patience*

Patience (center) with friends in ministry, 2016

Preface

Before I begin my story, I want to say that I am convinced my survival and progress in life all happened because I have set my heart, with God's help, to help prevent history from repeating itself. My desire is to leave a legacy of words and memories and faith.

I share my story to preserve a record of the ordeals I endured as a girl child and adolescent in West Africa. I am writing this piece to shame the devil and to show the victory God gave me to overcome my shame, rejection, and fears of writing this book.

This may be the only book I am able to write in my lifetime. I am grateful to God for the miracle that I am alive—and you know what else? *My dark night of terror is over!*

Dedication

This book is dedicated to the Holy Spirit, my mother's children including my brother who passed away in 2008, and my children Moise and Marie-Noel.

Contents

1   **The Dark Side**

"Good morning Patience, I want to let you know that State will be here today," said my unit manager. It was 7:00 a.m., and I was preparing to begin what was going to be a busy day of nursing.

"State," is a word to describe the presence of representatives from the State Monitoring Board. It could be anywhere from one to four or more persons from the state during an investigation (or just a visit) to a nursing facility. When State is around everyone should be busy with work, working intelligently and carefully without breaking rules. We are also be expected to work together to help do things like arranging furniture, organizing shelves, maintaining safety and efficiency, and ensuring no one's privacy is violated. At the same time, we maintain optimum care to residents and patients.

Bridget, a large and intimidating coworker, stormed up to me. "Where is my back pack?" She demanded. (She normally kept it at the nursing station.)

"It has been put away by the unit manager," I replied.

Bridget snapped angrily. "I always keep my things here, I don't care who moved it, I want my bag!"

Her instant outburst gave me chills that ran down my spine froze me inside. Finally, I was able to say with a very low and meek voice, trembling, "Have I said anything wrong? What did I say wrong?"

Bridget stormed off and I began to follow in her direction, even though I was in shock and feeling frightened. She continued down a long hallway and turned out of sight. "What in the world just happened?" I asked myself.

Slowly, my fright and meekness began to turn into anger. I began to blame myself for not standing up to her. Immediately I thought, "No! I should not let this happen again!" I was ready to let all hell break loose on her.

Twenty minutes later, Bridget walked up to me. "Patience, you still don't know me do you? This is the way I talk and behave. I am loud!"

I replied, "Bridget, since the day you started work on this unit, you have been hostile to me. I am ready to put an end to it!" She just turned around and walked away.

Bridget's imposing size and harsh personality as she yelled at me immediately brought a flashback to my mind, almost like a movie. I remembered and I felt the way I did years ago when I was standing face to face with Tina, my half-sister, shortly before she beat me up. In my flashback, I was reliving my fears, feeling chills and fright, looking at Tina like the sight of a giant Anaconda snake.

Growing up in Nigeria, I was very tiny and weighed much less than every other child in my age group. As a result, I suffered endless beatings from my classmates and family members.

I was born into a polygamous family. My father had many wives and children. My mother was the fifth wife, living in the house with her five children, among other children who were my half siblings. Some of my father's children lived there and some did not. It was a normal polygamous family where sometimes there was anarchy, and sometimes it was happy and cheerful.

Our father lived as a man of honor—a man who was well known in the family, around the community, in the city and in the state at large. He was a popular and famous man. After serving in the Nigerian Army, he became a famous magician and musician who everyone loved and feared.

I was the tenth born of my father and the second born of my mother. This put me in a good position with my brothers and sisters as a typical African family. But like every other family, whether polygamous or not, there were some individuals who either did not agree with me, or just plain disliked me.

My parents lived in a house the whole family shared at the Government Reserved Area (GRA) in Benin City, Nigeria. I enjoyed living with my parents, brothers, sisters, uncle and aunt. We were a happy family even though it was a polygamous family. I was the 10th child out of 16 children and most of the time we all lived in harmony.

Every holiday, my father would take my brothers, sisters and I to my maternal village in Orhionmwon Local Government Area to spend time with our extended family. We had good family time together with our cousins. We went to the farms, cultivated, harvested, and hunted. We cooked, milled, and raised different animals. Village life was very different from city life and we loved it.

Every August was our favorite festival of the year; the "Ekaba" festival where all sons and daughters of Orhionmwon from all around the world attend. *(Orhionmwon is a Local Government Area of Edo State, Nigeria. Its headquarters is in the town of Abudu.)* The festival was beautified with masquerades of different colors, each of them having significant meanings and representations. I could not wait to go to the village every year.

From the back left: Father, Irene, Oduwa, Mother.
Front Left: Patience and late brother, Ebenezer.

During our stay with my grandparents, neighbors and friends came to the house, and upon seeing me, they did not need to ask who my father was. In amazement, they would say, "Oh my goodness, you look so much like your dad!" I was elated to have a resemblance to my father, who was my role model.

Back home in the city my family would watch Indian movies together on Friday nights, even though the kids were not supposed to be allowed to stay up past 9:00.

I never went to kindergarten or elementary school. My mother taught me English and Arithmetic at home. My father would give me money to get newspapers from the newspaper stand on the street and I would read it aloud to him and explain what I understood. I was allowed to start primary school later.

2 Intimidated and Fearful

One day, my parents decided that I must go live with a family member to help out while I was in Primary 2 (attending Ebenezer

Ebenezer Primary School

Primary School). Sending me there to live took away the joy and happiness I shared with my family. It marked the end of Friday night Indian movies, and separated me from the relationship I had with my siblings. It stole my childhood away from me. I felt frightened and rejected. But I was not allowed to question their actions or disobey. Culture forbids such actions and attitudes.

"Patience, get up, put your clothes in a bag now," my father ordered me.

"Father, why? Where am I going?" I asked.

"Your father wants you to go live with your aunt, to help her," my mother replied.

"OK Mummy," I replied. I was obedient to them.

My aunt's home was not far away from my parents' home. My aunt was a strong disciplinarian and educator. With her, I enjoyed and developed a love for birds and poultry.

But my experience at the place became negative quickly when

they found out I wet the bed at night. Bed wetting was an ugly experience I dealt with growing up as a little girl. It brought me shame and disgrace. I tried to stop, but little did I know it was beyond my control. As a result of this situation, the hiding place for  me and my clothes became the store house for the sawdust used on the poultry floor to reduce the odor of bird waste. It was located on the rear end of the large poultry house. Because of the bed wetting, I was forced to live in the sawdust storehouse. I spent many nights crying for my family. It was a scary and lonely place for a little girl.

After 3 awful years in this building, I was in Primary 6 at school. My mother decided to take me home with her because the conditions were so very poor. I felt relieved but also frightened. Would my father accept me back into the house, or would he send me back? Would he be angry? Would he be hurt Mother?

My family had moved from GRA to Sapele Road, which was about 9 to 10 miles from the Primary School. This was my father's newly built home behind Grandfather's house. Grandfather was more than 100 years old. We lived there so that mother could care for him since he was so old. I had to walk all 9 miles to school every day to finish up my primary education and head to Secondary School.

Not long after I returned home to live, Father took me to yet another family in the same city.

"Patience, you need to get your bag of clothes in the car because you are leaving today," my father said.

"Mummy, where am I going?" I asked my mother.

"My child, your uncle needs your help around the house, so your father wants you to go live with him and his family."

In grief and fear I packed my little belongings and Father dropped me off.

This home was part of a large compound where my 3 uncles lived with their families and children. Everyone had their separate apartments, but shared the same courtyard and a communal kitchen. I lived with one aunt and uncle and was happy for a little while. But my happiness did not last for long.

One day after school, I was hungry and waited for my cousin to dish me up some food. I had just gone to the courtyard, which led to the kitchen area. My cousins who lived in the flat next to ours came out to meet me.

"Come here!" they shouted.

"What have I done?" I responded.

"Who asked you a question? We told you to come closer!" They shouted as they walked closer and closer towards me. Before I could react all of the girls pounced on me. They were a family of 8, father and mother, four girls and 2 boys. I was a tiny girl and so I feared the bigger people. My cousins were on the bigger side and they pounced on me, beating me until I was deeply wounded. When I was finally able to get free, I ran into my immediate apartment for safety, trembling and wounded.

This was the beginning of everyday beatings for the rest of the months and years I lived there. My life became a living hell and there was nothing I could do to get myself out of it. I lived with the beatings and ate my meals while I cried. No one ever listened to my cries, looked at my wounds, treated me, or even advocated on my behalf for my father to take me home.

The only person who tried to stop the beatings was the girls' big brother. He felt bad for me all the time, but he wasn't around very often. I starved most of the time because I could not go out to the courtyard or kitchen to get food, in fear that I would get caught and beaten. If I had to go out for any reason, I would peep out through the door holes to check the surroundings before I could run (or tiptoe) to get to wherever I needed to go.

One day, I was very sick with a fever, and I begged to go home. Nobody listened or cared. Another day, I begged to pay my mother a visit. Again, nobody listened or cared. Sometimes my father would be present in the compound. I would plead with him to help me and take me home, but each time he refused.

Another time I saw my mother in the compound. I cried and cried telling her, "I am going to die before you know it! Please, please take me home with you!" My mother could only plead to Father on my behalf. She could do nothing on her own without Father's consent because of culture and tradition. She asked me to go back with my aunt, and she would plead with Father to come rescue me. I cried, choking back sobs as I returned, thinking "I will never be free. I am going to die." I went back there knowing in my little girl heart that all the pain and the horror would be over when I died.

I was still there at 12 years of age when I began my first year of Junior Secondary School (JSS 1 - or high school) at Oredo Girls' School. I loved the purple and white uniform so much. It was my favorite of all my clothing.

Soon after I started school, I joined the French Language Club, the Nigerian Red Cross Society, and the Christian Union - Oredo Girls' chapter. School was a fun place where I felt good about myself. It was also a place of solace for me.

Every year, schools organized inter-house sport games featuring parades, running, high jumps, and other exciting games where there were many invited guests and spectators. Green House was my favorite inter-school sport team where I was featured in the parade, high jump, and sometimes, running races. I especially enjoyed when I was chosen to watch for and take care of injured students.

Joining the French club in my school opened the way for me to lead the team to inter-school, state, and national competitions in Jos, Plateau State. I memorized and recited poems, and was featured in the play and cultural dances.

I attended the "Alliance Francaise" classes situated inside the ministry of Education, Iyaro, in Benin City for extra French lessons. I learned to read, write and speak French fluently. All these gave me a source of pride and a sense of purpose and was a source of joy in my life!

Joining the Red Cross sparked my interest in becoming a nurse. The desire burned in my heart and gave me purpose. During my lunch hours, I would go from one classroom to the other soliciting for donations of used clothing and other items on behalf of the Red Cross for disaster victims. After school hours, I organized and taught first aid classes. During the holidays, the Red Cross would hold camping meetings for up to a week to teach and certify and equip volunteers to help disaster victims.

There were times when doctors, nurses, and government hospital staff went on strike, because they did not receive salaries for 6 months or more. During the strikes, nurses, doctors, and hospital workers walked away from the hospital with patients lying helplessly in their beds! The Red Cross would be dispatched to the hospitals to help clean up and care for abandoned patients who were still in recovery. As members of the Red Cross, we were assigned and took turns caring for the patients until the strike was called off. I even had the opportunity to clean up or stitch up surgical wounds that were grossly infected, because the patients had been abandoned for days before we were able to be assigned to help.

I already saw myself as a nurse. With great pride and joy I wore the NRCS white dress, which looked just like the dresses of fully certified nurses. I went to annual camps for days with the group, got promoted, and got deployed.

I knew I wanted to be a nurse and loved how nursing care put a smile on people's faces. Besides nursing, I joined the Christian Union, which met every Wednesday after school. Students gathered, sang, prayed, and shared the word of God together for about 2 hours. The best part of it was joining the other schools once a year for a students' convention, held at a sister school close to my house. This made me a strong Christian and I wanted to preach and be used by God through the ministry of healing, leading the Christian Student Fellowship group, and ministering to students.

I led the assembly prayers, preaching, and the national anthem in the morning before classes. I loved the Lord, and my desire was to help others both physically and spiritually.

School was good for me! At the end of the first term, I came out in first position in my class which started the trend of coming out in first position at the end of every term. During school I was loved and became the envy of students and teachers. It felt good to have this blessing in my life.

Once my classmates noticed I came out on top of the class, my great joy was suddenly plunged into fear and sadness yet again. I began to receive threats before and after exams and tests. Some of my foes were classmates, including a set of twins. These twins had been my best friends until one of them decided that it was time she stopped being friends with me. She forced her sister to go along with it. At the end of the school day she waited with her sister, and on the way home she would beat me up. Her twin sister would beg on my behalf, but to no avail.

The other person I feared was a family member. One day, in my year 2 (JSS2) of Secondary/High school, I had just gotten my report card. Coming out in the first position in my class, I was rejoicing and jumping joyously all the way home. I went my usual route from school to home. Between the two streets leading to my house was a connecting path which was a shortcut. I got to the beginning of the shortcut and I stopped. There was my half sister Tina. Joyfully, I broke the news of my success to her. But I quickly understood that she was not there for my success. She descended on me and beat me until I bled from injuries to my knees and hands. I was shocked to my core. Why did people hate me for doing well?

That day was the beginning of the worst days—2 to 3 YEARS of repeated beatings after school. School had always been the place I

Oredo Girls' Secondary School classroom

could feel good about myself. Now I had nowhere safe and happy to give me something good in my heart and mind.

The next term, I had just received my report card and as usual I was jumping home joyfully when all of a sudden, I froze at the exact spot where I was always attacked. Once again they descended on me and beat me up. On and on it continued. Sometimes, I would be in the company of my sister and other times, I was alone. Onlookers and neighbors did what they could do, but it was little help to stop the beatings.

Some may wonder why I did not report it or say something to my parents. I actually did say something to my father one time. He told me, "Stop crying, I will go and tell them to stop beating you."

"Thank you daddy," I replied, still crying, shaking and staring at my wounds.

I ended up regretting the decision to tell my father, because it just made the beatings worse. So I decided to keep it all to myself and deal with it myself. From that day on, I would either cry my eyes out whenever it was the end of term, or try never to show that I was happy on my way home. I felt like death was near. I decided it was destined for me to go through all of this to become strong and never give up in life.

Finally in April 1990, I was too scared to go home after school, so I laid on my classroom bench and slept. At 5:00 p.m. I heard the school gate open and saw my mother come to the classroom with the gate man to look for me. The gate man had told her there was no one in the school compound, because he did not know I was still there, hiding and sleeping in a classroom.

"What are you doing here. Why aren't you home?" My mother asked, surprised.

Trembling, I replied, "Please mother, forgive me, don't beat me. I was afraid of walking home. I was afraid to be beaten again. So I decided to sleep here in school."

My mother gave me a hug as I could not stop crying. I felt so relieved that she was not mad at me. She took me home immediately and she promised not to tell my father where I was found and what I said about my half sister.

3 Repentance and the Role of the Church

At this point in time, my father had put my mother away because she had just repented and given her life to Jesus. No one in the family would help my mother with a place to stay because she was now divorced.

My mother and my brothers and I decided to move with her to her brother's abandoned home at Upper Sakponba Road. The house was the last house down the road that led to a gigantic moat. One day, it rained so heavily that the moat filled up and flooded the whole area. We were all terrified, climbing on the top of the tables to avoid drowning. It took about 3 days for the water to recede enough that we could at least sleep on the tables.

Mother worked as a ward maid at Central Hospital, but the pay was so low that it was not enough to properly feed us. Often we would only have enough for one small meal a day.

This was supposed to be my last year of school. I started missing school because there was no food to eat before walking more than 10 miles to get there, and there were no good clothes for me. My uniforms were ruined in the flood. Even though I was happy that I was no longer getting my daily dose of beatings, I really wanted to finish school and become a nurse. At this point, the vision and goal of becoming a nurse seemed far fetched, but the desire continued to flame up in my heart.

My siblings and I did all we could to help by selling bean cakes, maize, firewood sticks, and bread on the streets. With this money

Mother was able to rent one room for my brothers and sisters, and I was able to go back to school. I continued school for the remaining part of the year and finished high school, although I did not really make good grades.

At this point, relentlessly, we walked more than 10 miles to the only church we knew, an Assemblies of God Church located at Oni Street, GRA. My mother and I were loyal members. I was devoted to this church, and missing any service was highly discouraged.

Services were on Sundays, then Monday was Youth Ministry, Tuesday was Bible Study, Wednesday was Prayer Meeting, Thursday Choir Practice, Friday was Sunday School Preparatory class, Saturday Choir Practice and Sunday School, and Prison Ministry was Sunday after service. At my leisure, I prayed, went out preaching the Word of God on both small and large buses, and attended seminars and workshops which I enjoyed so much.

After about 3 years, my mother decided we needed to move closer to the church. She found a one room place for us on Boundary Road, GRA about one mile from the church.

My real journey with the church started when I gave my life to Christ in the beginning of my secondary school years. Having confessed Him as my Lord and personal Savior, I was baptized by my pastor at the Ogba river, Oko village in my town in Benin City.

The Assemblies of God Church, GRA branch in Benin became family to my mother when she began her Christian journey in 1988. Against my father's belief and will, my mother became a Christian. She was baptized, filled with the Holy Ghost (with the evidence of speaking in tongues) and began to frequent the church almost every day.

As word spread about her salvation and new life, she soon became a ridiculed member of the family. As kids, we would watch my mother being slapped, hit with shoes, insulted, and threatened to renounce Jesus. We cried, and begged on her behalf, but we were told to talk to our mother if we wanted her to live.

Everyone in the family either feared my father or highly respected him because he was the first son of a well known and influential family. He was called Captain de Solos because of his military status, and because he was a magician and a musician. His father was the high priest to the king. People of Benin kingdom believed in ancestral worship—which was a normal phenomenon. Father was a no-nonsense man, followed in ancestral worship and knew no other form of religion. As the 10th child of 16, my mother being one of the many concubines, my siblings and I were among the least liked and cared for.

After my mother's conversion to Christianity and baptism in the Holy Spirit, her prayer life intensified. Father wanted her out of the house and every child who professed to be on her side. At this time, after a revival service, I too met Christ and was baptized in the Holy Spirit. This church soon became my home church and my family too, just like my mother. Mother tried to live with dad no matter the persecutions, but was forcefully thrown out. Father tried to cut her with a cutlass sword on a Monday afternoon. Living without my mother became a norm, but only for a short time.

Soon after my conversion in the Assemblies of God church, the Lord blessed me with the gift of intercession and ministry. I joined prison and hospital ministries, planted churches in remote villages, preached the word of God in buses, cars, schools, and everywhere I found myself.

One Saturday morning, after a Friday all night prayer vigil and revival at the church, I arrived home. Father was very angry at me and said that I should not go back to church. I immediately fell on my knees to ask for forgiveness, but he refused and said, "I will only let you in my house if you stop praying and never attend church again." Since culture did not permit us to respond to our parents, I quietly went in the house and went to bed.

On Sunday morning, I got up and went to church as usual. I was so scared, but I bravely came back home. Father took out his gun from under his couch and pointed it at me. I fled outside in terror. I stood outside the house, still pleading with him. He came to the balcony and held up a native Benin iron piece called "Eben," which is a royal symbol. He cursed the day I was born and said, "I do not want to set my eyes on you ever again."

I ran away to my mother's home. A flood had just destroyed all she had left, even her clothing. Though mother worked as a ward maid at the famous Central Hospital in Benin city, the salary she earned could barely feed her 5 children. We would walk more than 10 miles to the church everyday, often times knowing that we would have nothing to eat when we got home. That did not stop or discourage us from our new found faith in God. I devoted my life to the church, preaching and intercession.

I remember walking back from school one day, very hungry, with absolutely nothing to eat. I felt like going out to preach the gospel anyway. Tired and hungry, I went out with no money to pay transportation, and started to preach the gospel of salvation in a big bus called Oyegun bus.

As I preached, I heard a woman say to the bus conductor, "Do not collect money from that preacher, I will pay for her." I heard another say, "I was going to pay for her, why don't I give her the money instead." I had passengers give me money on the bus and even though I tried to refuse, they gave it to me anyway. I had preached until 8:00 p.m. and went home. At home, I told my mother the story and when we counted the money, it was enough to buy food for the rest of the week until she got paid again!

Every day, I prayed and asked God, "Lord, what is my goal in life; what do You want me to do?" Sometimes I prayed in words that I understood, sometimes groaning, and other times words I could not explain. I fasted and prayed for God to save souls, saying things like, "Pharaoh's heart was hardened, not because he wanted to, but because You, Lord wanted to show Your mercy! Please show Thy mercy on these people." In dreams and visions, I saw many people, countries, nations, and tongues. I saw different colors of people going on a wide road, but with eyes focused on the sky, as though they were waiting, expecting, longing for redemption.

One day, after 3 days of dry fasting, I felt in my spirit to go out to Central hospital to preach the message of healing to someone. I was led to the rear end of the hospital and to a man who was admitted for tuberculosis. Although not certain who in particular this man was, I arrived at the open area full of beds, and preached with a loud voice and asked if anyone wanted to give his life to Christ. The man raised his hand—the same man I had seen in my prayers—and asked to be prayed for. I looked at him, all skinny and bony, looking very sickly and I was moved to tears. After having led him to Jesus, I laid my hands on him and prayed. I returned one week later to pay him a visit, and he was gone home, healed!

After that day's encounter, the passion to help the sick became so overwhelmingly great that I asked God to help me figure out if this was truly His will. I became more and more passionate and went to the hospital to preach and pray for the sick every Sunday after church.

Soon after, I joined the Nigerian Red Cross Society, Oredo Girls' chapter. I also became the Assembly and Health Prefects. All along I earned my teachers' praise, because I was one of the students that made them proud. By the age of 17, I had received my first aid, practical, and advanced first aid diplomas.

After high school, I wanted to become a nurse, but that sounded like a joke, because there was no way I could afford to go to college. As my passion grew for the sick, I was consumed about nursing. All I needed to do was find a way to go to the famous school of nursing in Benin City or Edo State university—but it cost a ton of money.

My mother started selling bread. We would walk every other evening (depending on whether we had good sales or not) about 10 to 15 miles, from where we lived on Upper Sakponba, to the bakery at Ekehuan road to buy bread. We carried the trays of bread on our heads as we walked back home, in case someone might want to buy some along the way. We tried to sell pap (tapioca made from scratch), corn meal, and anything mother could make and sell for money to feed us. At times the pastor's wife had us live with some well-to-do members of the church to help them with chores, so as to help my mother feed her 5 children.

After so many years in the Upper Sakponba area, my mother was able to move closer to the church into a one room flat in Boundary road, GRA. This made our life easier.

Then I met a young man in his 30's named Chucks (last name withheld). Chucks was a tall handsome young man from the Bendel Ibo tribe who worked as the manager of a bakery off Ugbor road, Benin. Chucks was a born-again Christian and child of God, but was not an Assemblies of God member. He lived a couple miles from the Assemblies of God church where I attended service.

Ten years prior, Chucks and I had met at an inter-denominational prayer meeting. He was interested in knowing me better, or better still to marry me. I feared talking about marriage with Chucks, because my church doctrine did not permit marriage outside the Assemblies. I told Chucks I wanted to go to school for nursing and then think about marriage, if the church will allow that. He did not mind sending me to school first, then talk marriage later.

After we renewed our friendship, on a Sunday evening, I had visited Chucks at his bungalow home in the evening. Afterward while I was on my way to get a taxi home, I saw a lady whose sister attended my church. I said "hi" and continued home. That lady told her sister that she saw me holding hands with Chucks—which was not true—and her sister reported it to the church. The Assemblies of God forbids an unmarried couple to hold hands. So, my crime was that I held hands with this brother who is not from Assemblies and he was unmarried and my crime was termed, "Appearance of Evil."

The following Tuesday was Bible Study. After the meeting, the deacons called me and told me what they had heard. I said I had done nothing with him, and that he wanted to send me to school and then marry me. All hell let loose. When the discussion became tough, they offered to pay for my school if I would let him go.

One of the deacons who was a lawyer asked me, "If we pay for your school, will you let him go?

I said, "Yes."

"OK," he said, "you will still be punished, then we will see what we can do."

The accusation of holding hands with Chucks was enough to discipline me and put me in the back seat. Now, "back seat" means a lot to an Assemblies of God member. It means one is separated from everyone and everything, spiritually and physically. You sit alone on the back bench behind everybody in the church where you are not allowed to shake hands with anyone or have any physical contact. Your offering is collected separately if you have any. You are unworthy at this moment.

When someone is being suspended or put in the back seat, the church, led by the pastor and elders or deacons, lay hands on the person to be suspended, pray and ask God saying, "Anything that is bound on earth shall be bound in heaven, so we bind her today.

From now on, in heaven and on earth, she's on hold."

After the given time passes, the person on suspension will come back up and the same prayers will be prayed to loose the said person and set them free from bondage of suspension and whatever holds them back.

The pastor, Rev. Ehigimetor, called me and told me that it was not him who wants this on me, but the deacons and elders. Because he did not have control of the church's decisions, he let them carry out whatever they wanted, even though he believed me when I said I was innocent. He encouraged me to obediently and humbly serve my suspension time in the back seat and be free. I cried and cried! Another betrayal and more wounds in my life that seemed so unjust and unbearable.

On Sunday morning, I did not want to be disgraced in the front of the congregation, so I stayed home. The church still prayed anyways. Every Sunday after that became hell for me. Going to church, believing I was bound in heaven and on earth, sitting alone, people looking at me like I was a prostitute and avoided me.

My love for Christ remained, but it felt different, like my life was in slow motion. My life in the church began to slowly deteriorate. I hated my church family, deacons and elders. My zeal and strength to help the church grow, work as a Sunday School teacher and secretary slowly died. A new day of sadness, loneliness, doubt, and lack of trust, began to creep in like the dawn. I felt it slowly growing. I knew it wasn't good, but I could not help it because I felt betrayed by the only family I knew.

Months went by and it seemed to me that I had been forgotten in the back seat. I would cry and cry, ask God to please forgive me and touch their hearts to set me free.

In the sixth month of my punishment, there was a three day revival service beginning on a Friday evening and running until Sunday morning. Rev. Edogiawerie was the revivalist.

After the Sunday service, I stopped him on his way to the car, crying and pleading with him to ask the church deacons to have mercy on me and release me. He asked me what I had done and I explained the situation. He called the pastor, the elders and deacons and told them that what I have been accused of does not deserve a 6 month suspension and he asked that I be released as soon as possible. The next Sunday, I was called to the altar and released. I was done. I left the church.

4   I Want to Go Home

Two weeks later, I met Aboubakar, a young man from the republic of Cameroon. He was in Nigeria as a Bible School student and was a student pastor at the time. Aboubakar was about 5 feet 8 inches tall, dark in color; a well-built young man in his thirties who hailed from a small town and commune of Foumbot in Cameroon.

Foumbot is in the west province of Cameroon and people of this Noun area speak many languages including French, Arabic, Bamoun, Bamileke and are mostly dominated by Muslims. Aboubakar, who was from a Muslim dedicated family, was a well known Islamic Imam and teacher before his trip to Nigeria as a bible school student. He smiled all the time. He was noticeable and the room would light up when he entered. He preached the message of hope, he prayed fervently, and spoke in tongues. He came to Nigeria, studied at All Nations for Christ Bible Institute, a school founded by the late Archbishop Benson Idahosa in Benin City.

His testimony was that he was a Muslim convert who was persecuted in his home country, but was privileged to escape persecution through some American Baptist church missionaries who sent him to school in Nigeria. Anyone who heard the testimony of Aboubakar gave thanks to God for rescuing him from Islam and the trials he had been through.

I told Aboubakar my own experiences as a Christian, my shortcomings, and what I thought I would like to become in the future. He promised to communicate with these missionaries on my behalf so that I could be helped.

Three days later, he stopped by the house to tell me the American Baptist church missionaries would like to help me go to school, but in Cameroon. When I asked why in Cameroon, he responded by saying that the Baptist Church has a nursing school and a hospital situated there, where they train nurses and treat patients at the same time. I jumped for joy! I was so very happy—not only because this was the beginning of my dream of becoming a nurse, but also because I was going to do the work of God with the Baptist missionaries in the French/Arabic/English country of Cameroon!

That evening, I could not wait to tell Mother my good news. Mother asked me if I thought this was a good idea. She was very concerned because a girl should not be alone with a man—it was not safe.

"Oh yes, it is a good idea. Remember I want to be a nurse and preach the Gospel and we do not have the means to make this happen. You work and can hardly take care of us, so please allow me to go and become a nurse and be back," I replied. Mother could not keep me from going to Cameroon.

Weeks went by and I held onto faith that I was going to Cameroon for nursing school. Aboubakar soon became a part of my family. Although he lived in the Bible school's dormitory, he came over to the house, hung out, ate, played, and prayed with us. He was always nice and spoke positively, but never spoke about his family.

Whenever he stopped by the house, he would tell me that he had good news for me—the good news was that he had spoken with the missionaries. I was always eager to hear him talk about the missionaries because I hoped they were going to help me.

One day he came and announced that he was ready to go to Cameroon.

"When do you leave?" my mother asked.

"Aboubakar says we leave tomorrow, in the early hours of the morning," I replied.

The next morning, mother prayed for me and gave me an amount of one hundred and fifty Naira (N150.00, which was equivalent to $10), because that was all she had. Aboubakar came to the house and we set off on our journey to Cameroon.

We took the first taxi from Boundary road where we lived to Ring Road and to Ikpoba Hill where we headed for the northern border between Nigeria and Cameroon. At the park, he warned me that we would not take the normal transportation like taxi or a bus because we do not have enough money for transportation. Instead, we would hop on big lorries (trucks) due to the fact that they were cheaper.

"I had the idea that the missionaries sent you some money to bring me to school—at least so you said," I said to him.

"Oh yes, but we need to make good use of it, because we could have some problems on our way," he responded.

Still happy, I did not care if I had to ride in the back of big trucks as long as I could get to Cameroon and go to nursing school.

We spent the first night on a truck and got to our first stop on the second day in Jalingo, Sardauna (local government area) of Taraba state, Nigeria. Aboubakar told me that I needed some rest because the journey ahead of us was a long one. We went to a round shaped house that was built with sand soil and roofed with bamboo sticks and palm leaves. As we knocked on the wooden door, a man, black and tall came outside, very happy to see Aboubakar. He hugged him and shook my hand. He invited us into his hut and gave us food.

That evening, together we decided to visit the Mumuye people. The Mumuye people live on the mountain, a walking distance from Jalingo town. It was a lonely path to a village of naked people. I never really knew there were still naked people in my country until then. I was surprised and excited to see them. They had no bra, pants, and were not ashamed to be naked. They seemed very innocent to me. Arriving at the entrance to the village, I could see them hiding behind their hut houses, scared to see people, especially people that were wearing clothes.

Example of Mumuye people.

We went to the center of the village and met a man in his mid 50s with a long beard and a piece of dirty and torn cloth wrapped around his waist to cover his front private part only. He was from Jos, Plateau state serving as a pastor.

"I attended All Nations for Christ Bible School in Benin city and graduated some five years ago," he said. This is the

Road conditions near Gembu.

same school Aboubakar was currently attending. "I got a call from God to come and bring the gospel of Jesus to these people and I have been here ever since," he added.

I was surprised to discover that this man left his wife and four children to preach the gospel in the village where their food, water, culture, language, and everything was different from others. He came here, learned the language and now he was in the process of translating the Holy Bible into their language. He became the translator to any group of strangers visiting the village.

I was thirsty and asked for water to drink. They fetched me some water and I looked into the cup. It was dark at this time, so I used my flashlight to look into the cup. I saw that the water looked very brown. Because they have no water in the village, they fetched their water from a hole which made the water brown. I pretended to have a sip, thanked them, and poured the water on the ground when no one was looking.

The pastor went out and called the village elders to exchange greetings and we sang and worshiped God in their language for about 30 minutes, then we bid them goodbye. The three of us journeyed back to Jalingo town and went to bed to get ready for the next day's trip.

The following day, we journeyed from Jalingo to the next town called "Gembu." I found the journey to Gembu a very interesting one. Although the distance between Jalingo and Gembu would normally take about six hours, the hilly terrain and sloppy roads make it harder to travel, therefore increasing the distance to about twice the amount of time.

Gembu, a town on the Mambilla plateau is situated about 5,000 ft above sea level. The terrain is so steep that one little mistake or problem climbing up the hill in a vehicle will cause the vehicle will roll backwards and fall into a ditch. So scary! Throughout the journey to Gembu, all I could do was to close my eyes and pray!

Mambilla area.

We got to Gembu later that evening and it was very cold. The people there spoke Bantu, Arabic, Fulani, Hausa, and other local languages. They were predominantly Muslims and cattle rearers.

Because it was a Sunday morning, we proceeded to a Baptist church nearby. Everyone in this church knew Aboubakar. They called out to him, "Pastor Aboubakar, welcome back!" The church asked Aboubakar to introduce me which he did saying, "This is sister Patience, she's a sister in the Lord who is going to Cameroon for studies."

The church warmly welcomed me. There was plenty of joy and jubilation, praising and singing songs to God, with instruments made from empty bottles, cans, drums of various kinds and anything that can make sounds. It was great!

They asked Aboubakar to preach since he was a visiting Pastor. He stood in the altar and preached. When he was done and the church closed, he was handed an envelope with some money inside and we were invited to have lunch at a member's house. We enjoyed that very much because we were so hungry.

After lunch, it was time to continue our journey to Cameroon. At this time, we were not at the border between both countries yet, so we had to journey to the border on foot. Aboubakar suggested that we should not waste any more time in Gembu, since the border was far away from town.

By nightfall, we arrived in the small village of Bommi and we headed straight to what was known as a motel. The motel was a mud house having many rooms inside. These rooms had locks on their doors, and beds also made from mud (red sand).

A man dressed in robes and a turban met us at the entrance of the motel. The man stepped aside with Aboubakar and talked while I waited in the cold. Both men behaved as though they knew each other. This seemed very strange to me, but I remained quiet.

After about five to ten minutes of discussion, Aboubakar came towards me and directed me to go into one of the rooms. A little surprised, I said, "What do you mean, are we sleeping in the same room?" He looked into my eyes, saying, "Oh, I forgot, I needed to get two rooms—but we do not have enough money to travel from here, I am just saying."

"Please, get another room, because I am not ready to share one room," I replied. He said goodnight, left the room, and I locked the door behind me.

At about midnight, I heard a knock on the door. I could not sleep because I felt afraid being there. I knew something was not right. I asked who was knocking and Aboubakar said that he wanted to have a word with me concerning our next step in our journey to Cameroon.

As I opened the door, he pushed his way in, locked the door behind me, and started to touch me inappropriately. I cried out, "Are you out of your mind? Pastor, do you realize what you are trying to do?" Aboubakar knew that I highly respected him as a man of God.

"I know that I am a pastor, but please I just want to touch you, I need you!" He was still trying to take off my clothes. At this point, I knew he was serious about sleeping with me, so I became firm and started to raise my voice. I happened to have an army utensil, having a combination of spoon, fork, and knife, inside my luggage. I quickly reached out to my luggage, brought out the knife and pointed it at him.

"If you touch me, I will kill you and if I can't kill you, I will kill myself!" I told him. With the knife pointed at him, he let go of me and took 2 steps back.

"You don't have to do that, Please let me touch you for once, please," He continued as he stepped towards me again.

"I will kill you, stop now!" I continued with a firm voice.

"OK, fine I will leave," he replied. He stopped touching me and left the room. I went back to bed and laid awake until dawn.

At 6:00 a.m., Aboubakar knocked on my door signaling me to leave for Cameroon.

"I am not going to go with you anymore!" I replied. I told him that after what happened last night, I did not want to continue the journey.

He said, "I really apologize for what happened last night, the devil used me and am glad you did not let the devil win. I need you to pray for me, because the devil wants to destroy me. Ask God for me, please." He continued, breaking down into tears.

After 20 minutes of crying and wiping his tears, he said, "Also, you understand that I do not have money to give you to go back home, so come with me and the missionaries will get you the money to go home if you still insist."

I forgave him and decided to continue on the journey with him. We walked for miles and miles, hours and hours, up and down steep hills through heavy brush, carrying our luggage on our heads. Finally I asked, "When can we take a bus or taxi? I am so exhausted from all this difficult walking."

"It is all forests, hills and valleys here now. We have to walk across these forests into Cameroon. That's how it works from here on," he said. I burst into tears. I was exhausted and hurting.

"We will be there soon, stop crying please," he said, wiping the tears from my eyes.

Here on the Mambilla hill, to the northeastern corner of the Mambilla plateau, is the Mambilla-Gashaka-Cameroon tri-point boundary zone with many villages. Villages there are found both on the hill tops and the valley bottoms relatively isolated from one another, especially during the rainy seasons when it's impossible for any motorized transportation or river crossings.

As we walked past the villages, the villagers came out to stare at us as though they had never seen people like us before in their lives.

After walking the whole day, we finally arrived at night to a pastor's house, which looked like a hut. A man and his wife came out to welcome us. They knew Aboubakar very well from the way they familiarly extended greetings and we were served food. Even though the food was strange, I forced it down my throat, because I was famished. I did not understand what transpired between Aboubakar and these two people. I prayed and fell into an exhausted sleep.

The next day, when I tried to get up and stand, I couldn't do it. I hurt everywhere in my body. I was in so much pain that I cried and cried. The couple gave me a walking stick, assuring me that I would be fine. They said it was nothing but pain from walking a long distance.

Even though I wanted to go back home to my family, I could not. I was not going to risk walking through those forests to get back to the motel or Gembu town. So I was forced to endure the pain as we continued our journey.

Foumban and surrounding countryside.

Foumban market.　　　　　　　　　　Foumbot market.

The next morning Aboubakar and I set out on our way to the Nigeria-Cameroon border. We walked from 4:00 a.m. until evening!

Finally, we arrived in a little village in Ngaoundéré. We boarded a land rover leaving to the next bus stop, until we arrived in Foumban.

In Foumban at about 9:00 p.m., he told me that we just have less than an hour and we will be at our destination—Foumbot town.

As soon as we arrived at the bus stop at the heart of the town (where the central market was also located), he got motorcycles, one for me and the other one for him. We mounted and rode for about 5 miles from the market square through some deserted roads. It was so dark that I never saw anything on our way except the lights from the motorcycles.

We arrived at a house all fenced around with flower trees. Immediately, a young man in his teens came outside and saw us, jumped, and ran back into the house to call everyone. People from the neighborhood, family members and friends came around to welcome us. Aboubakar has six siblings, 3 boys and 3 girls and parents all living together in that compound.

Even though two of his sisters were married and had children, they returned home whenever they had problems with their husbands. They were so young that after they had any issues with their husbands—if they were beaten or they were not provided for, they run away to take shelter at the parents' house. When their husbands come to plead and ask for forgiveness, or any time they were forced to go back to their marital homes, the sisters would leave with their children. This happened almost every week, so at the time of our arrival, the house was full.

Finally made our way into the house and sat in the living room. Shortly after that, a young man who was a hunter brought us a deer he had trapped in the forest. Immediately the family started preparing the deer. Everybody ate and there was lots of joy and merriment in the air.

I could see the wondering in their faces as they pointed at me, asking him who this was. I did not understand the language, as they did not speak French. They spoke their local dialect, called "Bamoun." After he finished his explanation, the people were very excited and began to give me hugs. I noticed the hug was not a hug for "a stranger," but a more familiar hug. I began to suspect he had told them something other than I was a Christian sister he was sending to school.

Aboubakar introduced his mother, brothers, and sisters. Later, he introduced his neighbors and friends all around.

The whole occasion ended at about 2:00 a.m. They set a room for Aboubakar and told us we would sleep in the same room. As soon as we entered the room, I discovered it had just one bed! My suspicions were confirmed! I was very uncomfortable and upset, knowing they have mistaken me to be Aboubakar's wife! I asked Aboubakar for my own room. He said we had to share the same room and bed since the house doesn't have many rooms, and that this was the only available one.

I began to question him, wanting to know when he would be taking me to the school to start my nursing studies. He explained that he had not seen his family for over three years, so this was a good time to stop by here, visit, and he'd take me to school after. He then promised to go to Bamenda the next day to make clarifications concerning the start date and the program and get my accommodations set inside the school. He said the missionaries were already waiting for me and they were aware of my presence in Foumbot.

He assured me there was nothing wrong in sleeping in the same bed. I laid on the bed and slept off immediately as I was completely exhausted from traveling. As I slept, he tried touching me and I told him to stop. I reminded him of how he had tried and failed at the hotel at the border, and told him my stand had not changed. He continued to try and make advances and I continued to resist. I told him I would scream if he did not stop. To my surprise he said I could go ahead and scream all I wanted because he was sure nobody would hear me in this mud house. Besides, he said, if I shouted, nobody would come even if they heard my cry.

"This is a Muslim community and if you don't act right, you could be killed—**they kill people like chickens here**. I am going to teach you what Muslims believe and you will realize that you have no other option."

He told me how influential he was in the community and that nobody would come to my rescue. As he spoke he was forcing his way into me, covering my mouth with his other hand. It hurt so much, but it dawned on me that I would not be safe if I continued struggling with him. Even though I cried and we spoke out loud, nobody came to my rescue. When he was done, he slept and I sobbed for hours. At that moment I developed hatred for Aboubakar.

In the morning, he tried to make me happy by taking me for a walk, and talked about how much he wanted to show he loves me and how much he wants to keep me. I told him that was NOT the reason I came with him, I did NOT want his love, and if he does not take me to Bamenda, I want to go home. Immediately his tone changed, and he acted like he felt remorse. He apologized for what he had done, saying, "Patience, I am sorry, it was the devil that made me do it, forgive me. Remember, I am a man of God, forgive me. I will take you to school."

Later that evening I asked him if he had spoken to anyone in the school or reached the missionaries. He said he had called and they said we should come there next week. I waited a few days and then asked him again when we were going to Bamenda. This time he said we didn't have enough money for transportation to Bamenda, and that the missionaries said they will be sending him some money.

This lingered for the next three weeks. He didn't touch me again because he had asked for forgiveness.

In that third week, I started to throw up and feel sick, especially in the morning. My breasts started to increase in size and shape, and I felt many changes in my body. I knew something had changed in me, and it dawned on me then that I was pregnant. Immediately I burst into tears. Aboubakar came into the room and saw me crying, he asked that we go for a walk, so I followed him. On our way he asked what was wrong and I told him I was pregnant and reminded him of what he had done to me. Surprised, he asked how I knew. I told him I felt changes in my body and that I was sick in the morning. He sat me down on a little rock along the road and said he was sorry it happened. I didn't know what I would do because in Nigeria I needed to get married before even going to bed with a man. I remembered how my church treated me when they thought I held hands with Chucks, and I felt afraid. I was quiet as I was filled with confusion.

He suggested having it aborted. I said no! I was keeping the child because I did not believe in abortion, and was not ready for an abortion which could lead to my death. He agreed to keep the pregnancy and because of this, he would go to my parents and family and tell them he was going to marry me. I told him I did not want to marry him and that I was ashamed of myself and I did not know what to tell my family, the church and everyone else. Then I told him I hated him. He begged me and told me he wanted the child so I should keep it for him. He also said this was not how he had planned it all, but that he had liked me from the beginning.

I was so emotional that I could not say anything as he spoke. His words and ideas kept changing, and I could not believe anything from his mouth as the truth. I dried up my tears and we went home.

As time went by it became clearer that I was not going to the nursing school. He continued to lie about the school. He told me things like, "The missionaries were in the United States... No one is in the administrative office because they were all on vacation," and so on.

Gradually I began to give up hope, trying not to think about the school as my belly gradually grew bigger and bigger.

In Foumbot, the first few months were not really bad, however I was too ashamed to try to go back home. I felt I was a disgrace to my parents, my family, friends, and to my church. So I decided to stay. I still had hopes of going to the nursing school in Bamenda because Aboubakar had promised that I would go there after the delivery. He promised that he would use the time before my delivery to meet with the missionaries and make other preparations. I never stopped praying.

At times I was taken to the farm where we worked and came back home with fire wood and food stuff to cook. It was not an easy time for me.

5 ◆ Your Name is Hajida

My baby bump was gradually protruding. There were times when I had mixed feelings about Aboubakar and what he was really going to do with me. Unbeknown to me, his father had suggested to his entire family the idea to change me to Islam and my name to a Muslim name.

One evening, Aboubakar called me to the living room and said, "I am tired of calling you Patience, we need to call you a new name which is not Christian."

"Why?' I asked.

"Because we want you to become Muslim," he answered.

"I do not want to become Muslim, I am happy as a Christian," I said.

Angrily, he stood up, and walked away, speaking in Bamoun language. Everyone began to take their leave one after the other until I was left alone in the room. Until this day, I never really understood what he had said that fateful evening, although I did remember his words, "they kill people like chickens."

One day Aboubakar's father told him it was time to give me a Muslim name and make me a Muslim. He planned to kill an animal to celebrate my change of name. Aboubakar told me what his father had said. When I asked him why, he said if a woman is married to a Muslim then she has to be a Muslim. Now I knew that I would not become a Muslim. I was born again and I was dedicated to my faith. Aboubakar told me that if I didn't become Muslim I was going to die. "Everyone here is Muslim," he said, "and if you don't become one, they are going to kill you. Nobody knows you're here. Nobody will come to help you." He threatened me in so many ways. I did not want to die like a chicken. Nobody knew where I was. Terrified, I asked what he wanted me to do. "You need to come to the mosque with my mother and the Imam would name you," he replied.

"What name do you think they are going to call me?"

He said "Aisha." Aisha is the name of the wife of the prophet Mohammed. I agreed to go to the mosque because of fear for my life and the fear of retaliation, but I said to myself, "Going to the mosque does not mean I am going to become a Muslim."

His father had told him to teach me how to pray so he put some water in a jug, they washed their hands and their feet. Aboubakar said, "I need to teach you how to pray and worship." I refused.

"You should know my father and the village by now, knowing that you will never go free if you don't obey them," he said as he gave me the jug of water.

I refused again saying, "I will not wash and pray. I can go to the mosque but I will not bow down because the Bible says I should not bow down to any image."

What a surprise! He angrily agreed! So, I did not wash or do the bowing. My stubbornness helped me!

We went to the mosque and we saw people sitting in rows, men separated from the women. The men sat in front and the women sat behind because Muslim men say women are dirty pigs.

I sat by Aboubakar's mother in a corner of the mosque. As they bowed I would sit down and not bow. I didn't know that the Imam was taking note that I was not bowing and I was not taking part in the worshiping. I was just there, observing. As a result of my non-compliance he decided not to talk about the change of name. When the worship was done in the mosque, everybody got up to go. I saw the Imam call Aboubakar and the father to a corner to talk to them, I left with Aboubakar's mother.

Later the family gathered in the living room talking in Bamoun language. I didn't understand what they were saying, but I knew they were talking about my disobedience, so I walked in the room, sat down, and looked at everyone in the eye. When they were done talking, Aboubakar came to the room and asked why I was not worshiping like every other person,

"You are this stubborn girl," he said.

I said, "Aboubakar, I am not going to bow down to any image other than Christ." Angry and yelling, he proceeded to hit me in the head and then to beat me up.

After that I was very scared all the time and I didn't talk much. Anytime Aboubakar got close to me I would tremble.

He told me "You are going to have that name whether you like it or not! You're going to be called Aisha whether you like it or not from today we will start calling you Aisha."

One day, Aboubakar's mother cooked and people came to eat. When I asked what they were celebrating, he said they were celebrating my name change from Patience to Aisha. I was crying a lot. Daily when they prayed, his father asked me to come pray with them. I would be brought out and forced to pray, but all I did was watch them pray, I didn't bow and I didn't pray with them.

After they had done this a couple of times, Aboubakar decided to teach me Islam. He said, "Maybe she doesn't understand. I need to teach her Islam." So he bought me a Quaran in French and English languages.

Each day in the morning I would walk about 2 miles to the farm, where I would work and bring back food stuff and fire wood. When I got home, while the mum was cooking, we would go in our room. Aboubakar would begin to teach me the Quaran. During these times, I was so tired that I was often sleeping and being inattentive, so he came up with a plan.

He said "We are going to write a book together. Since you understand and speak English, then we are going to write it in English." I asked what book it was. He said he had come up with this idea—since I was a Christian,we are going to write the book as Christians. We would write about the black stone in Mecca and about the Kaaba (the most sacred site in Islam). At that point, I was ready to know what Islam was, who Allah was and what the black stone represented so I agreed.

The first book was "Who is this Allah." Every morning he would sit me down and we would read passages from the Quaran just to know who Allah is. The book wasn't geared towards calling Muslims to be Christians or telling Christians to be Muslims. The book was just explaining who Allah is, what the black stone is.

I knew a little bit about Islam, and learned how to speak Arabic when I was learning French language in school. I learned Arabic as I worked on these books, comparing Quaran versions in French and English.

I spent a lot of time reading and working on the book, so for a while I didn't think about home and school anymore. It got to a point where he didn't have to yell at me, all he needed to do was to look at me with his bad/wicked glare and I would just behave myself.

When I was four months pregnant, Aboubakar's mother told him to take me to a place where they would check if I was really pregnant. Aboubakar then told her he was sure I was pregnant but she said my stomach was too flat. Then she said, "We shall see if she really is pregnant by the seventh month." To other people I didn't look pregnant because I was tiny and wearing big clothes. My breasts were normally large so they just thought I was not pregnant. Aboubakar knew I was pregnant because he saw the changes.

In the fourth month he told me he was going to Bameda and that he would return in two days. I agreed and he left. He was away for about three days. On the second day, his father decided to start maltreating me. He would yell at me. The house was small, and he would boil pepper in the middle of the house. The smell of it would go through the house, hurting my nose and throat, making me cough and sneeze. I ended up sleeping outside.

On the third day, Aboubakar came back and told me how happy the missionaries were, knowing I was there. He said he also told them I was pregnant, and they said I could resume school after delivery. I was so happy to hear that the school was still going to accept me even though I had a baby. On hearing how his father treated me while he was away, Aboubakar decided to find another place for me to stay.

One day Aboubakar said he was traveling again, and this time he was taking me to a pastor who was from the English side of Cameroon who had a church in Bamenda. He said he was going to be gone for about a week or two, and I had to stay with the pastor until he returned.

Bamenda, Cameroon

Aboubakar was now at this point both a Muslim and a Christian. At home he was a Muslim but when he left home, he was a Christian. To traditional people, he was traditional. He had so many faces and caps on.

He brought me to this couple who were pastors and he reminded them how wicked his father was and begged for me to stay with them because I was a Christian and I wanted to go to church. They agreed and even called him "pastor". Aboubakar didn't return for over a month.

Life in the Pastor's house was very strenuous; there was just the man and his wife. They had a big church with a lot of members. I would have to go up and down steep, muddy hills fetching water every day to fill drums. I would carry gallons, pots or bowls to fill up the drums.

Besides the strenuous work, I wasn't eating well because they didn't have enough to feed me with. I wasn't eating what I should be eating for my pregnancy, and went hungry most of the time. I still had to do all the work in the house except cooking which the wife of the Pastor did herself. Whenever they were fasting, I had to fast too. I wasn't treated as a pregnant woman. Every morning I needed to get up and fill the drums with water no matter how I felt.

One day, I started to have bad pains in my belly. The pastor and his wife then promised to take me to see a doctor around the corner, but didn't do anything until the third day. Then they told me to go to the house by myself and knock, and tell the doctor I was from Pastor Kami. I was in so much pain. I knocked several times with no response. I returned home to find that Pastor and his wife had left. They were always out visiting for evangelism or at the church.

The terrible pain continued, and on the seventh day I could not bear it anymore. I was getting weak and seeing patches of bloody discharge. Finally they knew it was serious and decided to take me to the doctor themselves.

The doctor wasn't going to treat me without a deposit of over one hundred Naira. The pastor and his wife were not willing to pay and I didn't have any money, so the doctor didn't do much. He asked what I did at home, and I told him how I fetched water from up the hill. He was surprised hearing I had to do all that work. He asked how many times I ate a day, so I told him that some days I took my only meal around 2:00, and some days I would fast with the pastor and his wife. The doctor became very angry and asked for my husband. I told him he had traveled and I didn't know where he was. Then the doctor became very quiet. I tried to confide in him, but he never helped me solve anything. He only said he would tell the pastor and his wife not to make me fetch water anymore—that it wasn't good for me at all.

After that day, I didn't fetch water anymore. The pastor's wife was unhappy with me as she didn't want to be the one doing the cooking and fetching of water. She treated me like I was not welcome.

One day, one of the church members named John Bosco came to me and he asked how I was doing. "I am doing fine," I replied, but he obviously didn't believe me. He said it didn't look like I was doing well, and that I looked like I wasn't eating. I started crying and told him the reality of my situation. He was very angry. At least one person knew what going on with me in that awful place!

The pastor, after hearing what the doctor had said, decided to give me some fruit to eat from time to time. I didn't really have medications to take at this point. I believe the pastor began to feel sorry for me, but his wife was very angry because I wasn't doing much housework anymore.

On the sixth month of my pregnancy, Aboubakar came back, and we both went back to Foumbot. When we got home, everyone was happy to see me except Aboubakar's father, who wanted me out of the house because I was a Christian who wouldn't become a Muslim.

I was not doing well because of complications with my pregnancy. I was having lots of pain and water coming out of me along with bleeding. I endured as best I could. I thought I was going to die because no one cared or was doing anything about it.

The pain became so unbearable one day that Aboubakar's mother told him to take me to a local hospital. Before we left, Aboubakar told me to tell people I was his wife; "Don't tell them you are not, because they are all Muslims and they don't like Christians here." I agreed. When we got to the hospital and I was given some injections, they said that I was not doing well with the pregnancy. I stayed there for a day and I was monitored. Then I was sent home. I felt better and the pain subsided, probably because of the injection and other medication I was given.

After one week at home, the pain returned and the discharge started coming out again. It was the first week of the seventh month. When the pain became unbearable, I was taken to the local hospital again, and the doctor said I wouldn't be able to carry the baby anymore. He monitored the baby and said I should have the baby immediately, because it could cost me my life if I continued to carry the pregnancy. He said there was too much damage that had been done. They gave me injections to help me deliver the child. This was on the last day of September. That night I thought I was going to have the baby. I labored for many hours. It was so painful and terrible, and yet the baby didn't come.

Finally at 1:00 a.m. on the first of October 1999, I delivered a baby boy. This was the seventh month of my pregnancy. After delivering the child, at first he didn't cry. They slapped him and did all they could and then finally the child cried.

"Congratulations, you have a baby boy!" The midwife told me. At that point, all the pains went away. They cleaned me up and in the morning, they said the child was doing fine. He was strong enough to go home and there was no need of keeping us in the hospital even though he was so little. So I came home with my little baby boy—my gift from God in the middle of my nightmare.

Friends came to visit. John Banya and Pastor Koumi came among others. I was in one room in the house. Aboubakar's mother helped me take care of the child. She would bathe the children and take care of him like a typical African mother. For the first and second day she also bathed me too. She would massage my stomach, clean me up and clean the baby up and after everything lay the baby down and we would start our day.

Aboubakar and his father decided to name the child Abdusalam. I was furious! My child would NOT bear a Muslim name. They ordered me to shut up, and told me that in Islam I have no right to say anything or give him a stupid Christian name.

I disagreed with them and said my child would be called Moses (Moise in French) because I gave birth to him in Pharaoh's house— that he was going to serve the Lord and he was going to be a leader. Immediately after I said that, Aboubakar said I was lying and I wasn't going to name the child. It was a tug of war.

During this time Aboubakar would leave the house and not return for many days. I never knew where he went. Then when he returned, he acts like we are "family" again.

6   It's Never Too Late to Pray

After Moise was born, I didn't feel like hiding from my family and my church anymore. I did feel bad about myself, but even so I thought that it would be good for me to call home so my family would know I am alive and that I'm OK and I have a child.

I told Aboubakar I wanted to go home since I obviously wasn't going to school. He argued that I was going to school, and that he had already told me that after I had the child I would go to school. I insisted on going home and I told him I would return. Maybe I would give the child to my mum and then come back. Aboubakar refused. When I asked why, he said because this was his child. I knew I was in trouble and at risk of being trapped there forever and I started crying.

Suddenly, he brought out some pictures and told me he had been to Nigeria. He showed me my brother, my sister and my mother. He said he had seen them and they sent their greetings. I asked if they knew I was pregnant and had a baby. He said yes they did and they were very happy for me. I struggled to believe him, but he said it was true. I told him the pictures were nice but I needed to visit home myself. That I want to see them myself and hear from their lips that they accept me and my child.

At this point I was still crying. He made it very clear to me that I couldn't go home anymore, especially now that I have his child. I was scared and heartbroken, and I knew that I was in big trouble. He made me promise him never to let anybody in the church or at home know that I was forced to come here against my own will. He told me I didn't have a place to run to or a place to hide. He also made me understand that everyone is afraid of the Muslims in this place, so I couldn't do anything—especially because I was a Christian. He said if I opened my mouth nobody would believe me and I could get myself killed like many other people before me.

After crying and grieving for days, I decided that I was going to shut up and wait on God to make a way. I believed that if it's really God I've been praying to and if God loves me, He would deliver me from Aboubakar. So I summoned the courage to live as if I was happy, so he wouldn't see anything wrong or have a feeling that I would run away. Even though I pretended to be happy in from of them, I still cried a lot in private. Moise was a month old and I still cried daily and I was barely able to eat.

One time as usual, Aboubakar traveled for three days. I had a vivid dream of a bag in a drawer in his room that contained some snake skin, a scorpion back, dead animals' bones, eyes and much more. I woke up praying and sweating. Then I went to that drawer and opened it. I saw exactly everything I had seen in the dream in the drawer in a black bag! I was shocked to my bones. I looked at the bag, I pleaded for the blood of Jesus, then I took it to the pit toilet and threw it inside.

When Aboubakar returned from his trip, he looked for his bag and didn't find it. He was furious and asked me about it. He told his parents and everybody that I threw his property away, then he came back and beat me up, saying I threw away his bag of spiritual things. When that happened I felt like I was in hell.

The next day, I saw two men walk into the house looking for Aboubakar. I told them to wait and I went inside to tell him he had visitors. He came out to meet them, then invited them into the little room that we were staying in. He asked me to take the baby out of the room and said he had something important he needed to discuss with the men.

I left the room and took my baby with me. He locked the door. The door had a hole in it so after about 15 minutes, when I didn't hear anything, I left the baby in the living room and went to the door to peep through the hole.

I saw Aboubakar sitting on a chair, and the two men sitting on the bed. I saw him take photographs and cut out the people in them. There was a large bowl of water there. He put the picture cutouts in the water, took a knife and began to stab the images on the pictures inside the bowl. I had seen such things done in African movies so I continued to watch.

When he was done, I saw them make some prayers. As they walked towards the door, I ran back to the living room. He saw them off as they left, so I ran back to the room. The bowl of water was there on the floor but the pictures were gone.

Aboubakar came back and I asked him what they were doing in the room. He said they were praying. I felt troubled. I knew it was beyond ordinary and it bothered me for days. I didn't have the guts to ask him about it, so I just kept it inside.

Days later when I saw he was in a good mood, I asked him again about what they had done. This time I confessed that I had peeped through the door, and I told him how I saw him cutting images from pictures. He told me that before he left to Nigeria to attend Papa Idahosa's Bible school, as a student pastor, he used to be a spiritual leader to people around here. He said he used to be an Imam and that he had a black bag that he carried. As a spiritual person he went to graveyards and slept for days because he needed to communicate with the dead on behalf of people. He gave a detailed explanation of all they had done and told me that the men had come to get someone off their back. They owed someone money they couldn't pay back, so they came to kill him by rituals so the man wouldn't be able to ask for his money.

I felt limp with shock. I was very surprised at what I was hearing. I asked him if he had ever really given his life to Christ or not—and what exactly had happened in his spiritual life. I asked him, "Aren't you really a pastor after going to Idahosa's school?" He told me not to ask him that and he wasn't going to answer. From the look he was giving me, I didn't dare ask further.

When those two men visited, they brought about eight fresh fish for him. He gave me the fish and asked me to cook them. I refused and told him I didn't want to be a part of the cooking or eating of the fish. I was afraid of those men and their strange practices. So he gave the fish to his mother.

After about three days, the men came back and rejoiced that the person they had wanted to kill had died! At that point, I thought that even if I couldn't escape, I could be very prayerful so he wouldn't be able to kill me too. So I began to fast and pray often and I began to cry more about going home. I couldn't hide my emotions from him, and the more I cried, the angrier he got at me.

When my son was about 2 months old, Aboubakar noticed I wasn't eating and that I was sick. I couldn't stop crying daily, so he decided to take me home! His parents also convinced him to take me home. I thanked him as this news made me very happy. We started the journey when Moise was a little over three months old.

As soon as we set out on the journey, Aboubakar said, "You have to promise me you will come back with me to Cameroon." I agreed because I wanted to get home so badly. So, I lied! We started by taking a bus going to Foumban village in the morning and at dusk, we were in the North on our way to Ngaundere. We crossed the border jumping from one range rover to the other until we were in Gembu town, Nigeria.

The central mosque of Gembu, Nigeria

Aboubakar pointed and said to me, "There is a mosque over there. That is the central mosque. Go there and let them know you need money to go to Delta State. Do not tell them you are from Edo state or they will have you killed because they do not like Christians." I replied, "You never told me you did not have the money to take us back home!"

He responded, "I am not supposed to tell you everything. You wanted to go home so YOU need to come up with the money for transportation." Again he warned me not to declare my name, religion, or where I am from. He said if I did not follow his directions, the child and I would starve and that he would be in a corner watching every move and step I took. I was stunned! I thought for a few minutes as he continued to beckon on me to proceed.

Having no choice, I went to the mosque asking to speak with the Imam. I was told he had gone home, and someone took me to his house.

As soon as he was told that this woman with her child were outside waiting to see him, he hurried outside and greeted me with a curious look on his face. I told him my name was Patience and I needed his help to go to Benin City. I was so desperate that I was ready to spill out all my problems and ordeals until he asked if I was a Muslim or a Christian. At that moment, I stopped and thought, "Maybe, I should not say anything and just obey what Aboubakar told me to."

I responded, "I am not a Muslim."

He said, "Do you want to be a Muslim?"

I answered, "That is not why I am here, please help me."

He had me come into the compound that he shared with his wives and children. I followed him in, shaking with fear. One of the wives gave me dinner, water for my son, and let me take a shower. After my shower, they showed me where I would sleep. I obviously wasn't leaving there that night!

The next day, I was told the Imam wanted them to teach me to pray. I sat there thinking, "What can I do to escape?" I perceived that the Imam wanted to keep me as one of his wives.

By the third day, I had started my escape plan. It was too difficult to leave the compound and the area without being noticed. So I targeted the time when everyone would go to pray. The fifth day, at night, there was a festival celebration in the heart of town and while everyone was planning to attend, I was planning my escape. I decided to leave without my luggage before anyone could suspect what I was really doing.

At 10:00 p.m. all was quiet. I looked everywhere in the yard. Seeing no people, I started to go towards the entrance of the yard. One of the wives looked outside her door, saw me and called out, "Where are you going?"

"To the festival," I replied.

She said, "You should have told one of my daughters to take you because it is not good for you to be alone."

I replied, "I will be fine."

She told me to leave my son there, but I refused to leave him behind. She was not happy that I disrespected and disobeyed, but I walked quickly, approaching the gate. As soon as I was outside the gate, I looked down the hill and saw no one except a few young men who just stared at me.

Moving quickly, I took every corner that seemed close to me. Finally, my heart pounding, I got to the car park. Aboubakar surfaced from nowhere! I knew immediately that he had been following me. He asked me why I left. I told him that I did not want to be married and changed to Islam and I did not want to die.

"Please take me home!" I pleaded. We slept at the car park and started our journey to Jalingo the next morning.

As soon as we got into Nigeria, we went to a place called Ring Road. I was so happy that I was going home, but in my heart I had decided to escape from Aboubakar as soon as I got the chance. As though he read my mind, he decided to stop and switch to a different taxi to go to Boundary Road where my mum and siblings were living. As soon as we stopped to switch taxis, Aboubakar took the baby and blocked me from getting in! He said he was going to take the taxi alone with the baby, while I take another taxi. When I asked why, he told me in French language that I had better shut my mouth. He said that he was going to bring the baby to the house, and if I ever say anything about the child to anyone, I would never see my baby again! At this point he was already inside the taxi. He further told me to remember the kind of person he was.

"I don't get what you mean!" I screamed. He threw some money at me and commanded the taxi man, "Drive! I will give you directions later!" They took off at high speed, and before I could react they had gone out of sight. Horrified, I picked up the money and quickly took another taxi.

When I got to my house, Aboubakar wasn't there. My family

came out and greeted me—my mum, my sister and everyone came rejoicing, as they thought I had died. I went into the house feeling frightened and confused. My mum noticed I wasn't happy and kept asking what was wrong. I kept telling her I was okay, but obviously she didn't believe me. I couldn't say a word because Aboubakar had told me I wouldn't see my child again if I said anything.

I was so terrified. I knew Aboubakar had lied about everything. My baby was only 3 months old and I didn't know where he had been taken to or if he was OK. I was panicking inside and terrified. Even though my heart was breaking, I didn't say a word about it.

I didn't see Aboubakar for another 2 weeks. When he finally showed up, I asked him urgently where my baby was. He asked if I had told anyone, and I said no. I pleaded with him to have my baby back. He said as long as I kept my mouth shut, I would see my child again. He said it would happen in HIS timing and he would let me know. I tried to find out where my baby was, but he refused to talk any further. I begged him several times to let me at least see a picture of the baby to be sure he was still alive, and he agreed to get me pictures.

Aboubakar left often. One month passed, and then two. When he finally showed up, I continued my plea to see my child. He finally brought me pictures after three months and I was devastated. I begged him to take me to my child so I could at least hold him and again he refused.

At this point I became furious and asked him what he wanted from me. He said nothing other than me keeping my mouth shut. He said if I said one word to anybody about my baby then I would never see the child again, so I agreed to keep my mouth shut. Now my child was growing without me, and I didn't know where he was! I was so hurt and afraid. All I could do was cry and pray, begging for God's help.

When the child was seven months old, Aboubakar came to me and asked if I still wanted the child. I quickly said yes of course! He gave me some money and an address and told me to go to the border through Aba to Abakaliki to wait for him at the address. I quickly agreed.

I asked if he was going to give me my child there and he said yes, so I told my mother I was going to travel. When she asked where, I told her Aboubakar was taking me back to school. She asked if I was sure, because somehow she felt something was wrong. I convinced her and left. I hurried to the border where he had arranged for us to meet.

Aboubakar finally brought my little son to me in a hotel. Before I had time to rejoice, he told me he didn't come to give me the baby, but to take me and the child back to Fombout. He then said he had allowed me to see my family and that it was time for me to come back with him. He went on to say that he hoped I knew we were at the border and that nobody would help me. I was trapped again. I asked him what he wanted from me, but he didn't say a word. I couldn't bear to leave my son with him, so I went with him back to Cameroon.

When I finally got my son back, I had begged to go home, but of course Aboubakar refused. He gave me two reasons I had to go back to Cameroon. First, he knew he had wronged me, but it was for my own good and for my future so I could to go to nursing school. Secondly, he said I should work on the books we had started, and when I was done I could go home. Terror made my decision for me. I consented and followed him back to Fombout.

This time, our route was through Abakaliki and Afikpo. Arriving in Mamfe in Cameroon, he ran out of cash and said, "I do not have enough money for food or transportation for you and the baby.

I need you to say that you are my sister once we get to the Baptist church on the hill."

During the elders' meeting, Aboubakar told them that as a Baptist pastor, he needed their help and introduced me as his sister. Although the elders suspected this was a lie, they could not really prove it. We lived in Mamfe for about one month while he tried to find money for us to return to Foumbot, and then Bamenda for nursing school.

Once we finally arrived in Foumbot, we received a large welcome from the people including his family. We stayed in the same room as before.

Days passed and we were trying to settle in, though his father was angry that I was still a Christian and that I had not changed my name to Aisha. Aboubakar's father told me he was giving me one last chance to do it on my own or he would have to use some force. I did not reply.

Days passed and I continued to read and write the books which made Aboubakar happy. I thought things seemed to be going well. That is until the day his father told me that he had given me enough time to decide on becoming a Muslim. Since I was not doing that, he threw my clothes and the baby's clothes outside at night. I put my baby on my back, picked up my box and walked away, having no idea where I could go.

Aboubakar ran after me and told me he had a place I could stay. Again I asked Aboubakar why he wouldn't let me go home and he said he didn't have money for my transportation home and he was looking into going to school. He told me of his brother and his friend who was a policeman who was married with two wives and children. He said I could stay with them for a while until he is able to get me a place in the school.

We then walked about 5 miles up and down steep hills. Aboubakar didn't help me carry the box or the baby. I had the box on my head and the baby on my back all the way to the house. We arrived at night and man welcomed me into his home.

Aboubakar told me as he was leaving, "You should understand that these people don't care about what you tell them, and they won't believe whatever you tell them. They believe me and you could get yourself killed." He went on to make me understand I was a total stranger in that place. I believed all those threats from Aboubakar so I kept my mouth shut.

I lived at the policeman's house for about three months, pretending to be happily married to Aboubakar, but it was a life of pretense. Thankfully, they were very kind to me and my baby.

Once in a while Aboubakar would come over while I continued working on the books. He told the Christians he was writing the book because he wanted to convert Muslims to Christians, and told the Muslims he wanted to convert the Christians to Muslims.

Working in the house, taking care of the baby and writing the book wasn't easy, but I had to do it in the hope that someday Aboubakar would let me go home.

7 ◈ Get Rid of Her

After three months living in the policeman's house, Aboubakar came with his mother and told me his father wanted me back and was sorry for sending me out of the house. The policeman also begged me to go with them, even though I did not want to.

Aboubakar gripped my arm tightly, took me aside and whispered in an angry voice, "You need to keep your mouth shut—say nothing to anyone. You need to smile and be happy. These people, I know them. If you try to tell anyone anything, they will not believe you because they would not think I am doing anything wrong." I believed him in fear for my life and my son's life.

"That's fine, I'll do just that," I replied. He was always there beside me to make sure I did not talk to anyone. When he left my side for even a short time, he would come back quickly and ask, "Did anyone talk to you; what did they say? What did they ask you? What did you say?" Somehow I knew he was powerful in his own way, and I thought I had better play along. I believed him and obeyed him out of fear. I lived in fear every moment of every day.

Aboubakar knew many people in the service like the police and gendarmes (military police). People loved him and believed him, both Christians and Muslims. He was some sort of hero in their eyes. He had a testimony of growing up in a Muslim family. He read the Quaran, went to an Islamic school and practiced Islam to the core as a radical Muslim. According to his story, he became an Imam (Muslim pastor) and preached Islam, persecuted Christians and those who do not practice the Quaran.

To the Muslims, his story was that he is bait to Christians (meaning that he is in the church so that he can preach Islam to the Christians coming from their perspective, so that he can win them to Islam).

His story to the Christians was that one day God "arrested" him and he converted to Christianity. While attending a Baptist church, he met with the missionaries from the United States and they sent him to Bible school in Nigeria, owned by late Reverend Benson Idahosa.

The Muslim leaders liked him and gave him money. The Christians liked him and gave him money. He went to both church and mosque, and sat on the altar pretending to be a pastor. He preached during crusades in Foumbot, and sat and ate with all of them.

Because of his deception, I did not understand which people I could trust and whom I could not trust. It felt like everyone was the same as Aboubakar. I could not believe or trust anyone. I was completely on my own. So, I kept my mouth shut and followed along. I began to get used to that deceptive lifestyle, smiling, laughing, and joking around like it was normal.

Once we returned to the house, Aboubakar's father welcomed me very warmly and told me how sorry he was for asking me to leave. He asked for my forgiveness and said I could stay as long as I wanted because he wanted his grandchild around him.

So I stayed and went back to the farm to work with the others in the morning to get food stuff and firewood. When we returned each day, we bathed and then we cooked, after which I went back to my room to study and write.

Days and weeks passed. I kept asking Aboubakar when I was going to school. He always gave me excuses. I would cry because after all I had been through I just wanted to go to school.

Aboubakar had told me he wanted to marry me because he loved me. He asked that I forgive him so that we could be a family. I refused, but he kept pressuring me. He said he wanted to take me home and pay my bride price (payment by the groom or his family to the bride's parents). At this point he was wearing me down more. I began to believe him because I already had a child so I thought about forgiving him.

About this same time, news reached me that Aboubakar had other children. In Yaounde, he had two children. In Douala, he had two, and right near us in Foumbot, he had two more! Besides that, he was having a relationship with some woman who lived at the market square and the woman's daughter, who was barely 8 months old, was also his child.

One evening, another woman had come to the house asking for support for the children she has from him. That day, as I sat in the room, I heard them talking in the backyard. The woman was raising her voice, yelling, expressing dissatisfaction for the way she and her children had been treated by Aboubakar. Speaking in French, Aboubakar tried to tell her to lower her voice.

"You have abandoned us," she said.

"I did not abandon you, I have been busy," Aboubakar replied.

"Then you need to step up and take care of our children. Your son has been asking where his father is and I do not know what to tell him. Your daughter too. I am sick and tired of your lies!" She said. "I also heard that you have another woman, that you came with her from somewhere and she doesn't even belong to our people. Now, who is she and what is she doing here?" She asked.

At this moment, Aboubakar told her to come with him and they left to go elsewhere to discuss me. After about 20 minutes, I saw Aboubakar's family exiting the house to the corner of the street where

Aboubakar was talking with her. They gathered around her and it looked like they were pleading with her. That evening, food stuff was gathered and sent to this woman, and her kids. Many things like this happened, and I still do not understand it all, even to this day.

Finally Aboubakar told me we would go to Nigeria in three months. I thought maybe I was finally going to be free! I kept asking him how we would go and if he had the money. But there was a problem for me. In order to cross the border and go to Nigeria through the many check points on the road, I needed papers. My papers had expired. Aboubakar suggested we get married so I could get my papers. I was very angry, but felt I didn't have a choice but to marry him if I wanted to get back home. He wanted us to have a traditional wedding and a court marriage. I refused and insisted we have only a court marriage so we can get my papers and leave. At this point Aboubakar finally realized I wasn't the least bit interested in marrying him. I just wanted to go back to Nigeria.

Cameroon is heavily regulated and you can't just move around without an identity card. I wasn't ready to do a traditional wedding because it would mean I have to change my name to Aisha. Aboubakar wasn't ready to do just a court wedding. So the marriage was delayed because we didn't agree to which of the marriages we would do.

His solution was to force me to sleep with him again. When the second sexual encounter happened, I got pregnant again! This time I didn't realize it until I was about three months along.

At this point Aboubakar sees me as his property because I already had a child from him. Aboubakar was glad that I wasn't going back to Nigeria soon, since I was pregnant. I insisted on going back anyway, but he reminded me of how bad the roads were and how I could lose the baby due to the stress of traveling the bad roads. I didn't want complications so he convinced me to stay.

It hurt my heart and made me cry that I was pregnant again. I got angrier and angrier with Aboubakar and my sorrow increased. Aboubakar's mother begged me not to travel with the pregnancy, and every other person, including his father, threatened that I would die if I traveled with the pregnancy. I decided to stay after they promised to let me go to Nigeria once I had the baby.

The baby was due to be born on February 2nd, 2002. Once again I was very malnourished and lacked care. Once again I had to do farm work and study without good food to eat. At 7-1/2 months, my water broke. I wasn't taken to the hospital as Aboubakar said I must have the baby at home. I started bleeding and had other complications.

Aboubakar's mum told me to go to a old woman's house close to them to massage my breasts so that my child would be able to suck my breast and not die—as this was in their beliefs. I refused, and this made them angry. They got more and more angry for every single thing they wanted me to do that I didn't.

They told me, "You are on your own." Then they stopped paying any form of attention to me at all. I was left all by myself and I was bleeding. I thought maybe I could just go to the hospital by myself, but there was always someone watching me at every moment. So there was no way I was going to be able to leave the house. Even when I tried to lie to have a chance to leave they still found a way to keep me from going out.

After 7 days of suffering in the house this way, waiting for the delivery in terrible pain, I felt like I had to push. Aboubakar was there just looking at me. I cried out to Aboubakar's mum to help me. I was afraid I was going to die because nobody was willing to help me. I begged and cried for help for so long, that finally Aboubakar's mum asked him to go get a vehicle, saying I could not walk. It felt as though the baby was trying to come out.

After a while, Aboubakar came back and told us he couldn't find a vehicle. At this point I just prayed saying "Lord I know You won't leave me alone; please I need help". Then Aboubakar's mum asked me to try to get up and walk. I still felt like I needed to push. I got up and slowly I walked, taking one small step at a time.

Not too far away from the house we got to a little clinic. I got in and they looked at me. To my surprise I was told I wasn't ready to have the child yet. I told them no—I already felt like pushing the child. They told me it was false labor and gave me some other excuses. They said it was too early and the baby wasn't ready. They gave me some drugs and injections that stopped the contractions. The liquids I was expelling also stopped. They demanded I stay the night so they could keep an eye on me, and that they would let me go home the next day. The date was December 24th, 2001. I told Aboubakar and his mother I couldn't go home. I told them I would die if they sent me home.

Very early the next morning, I felt like pushing again. I was yelling for help. The nurses where looking at me as if I was being ridiculous and they didn't want to help. They felt I wasn't ready and that I was just shouting. I begged them, telling them I felt like I was popping. Aboubakar's mum decided to check me. She pulled off my clothes and she found the baby's head coming out! She shouted for the nurses. Four nurses came and put me on a bed. They held my legs and arms and yelled out for me to push.

On the 25th of December at 2:00 a.m., my daughter was born. They congratulated me and told me I had a baby girl. I was so relieved and happy for my new baby.

Just a few hours later we all went home with the baby. At home I was allowed to rest for about two days. Then I had to resume farm work.

At this point, I have two children, no school, and the books were still not finished. But I just had to get back home somehow, some way. I told Aboubakar over and over I was ready to go home.

"We will let you go home if you stop crying" he said to me. He said they were planning that we both go to Nigeria with the kids. But he said the kids and I needed paperwork. More deceptions.

When Noel was born, naming her was an issue. Aboubakar's father said she would be called Hadija, but I refused and said she was going to be called Marie-Noel—which means Merry Christmas in French. When Aboubakar's father heard it, he became furious. Aboubakar lied and told him her name was Hadija so that I could go home. I hadn't told Aboubakar I had written Marie-Noel in the papers. I tried not to be too stubborn, and I tried to do what they wanted because I knew I couldn't fight against them. They kept calling her Hadija but unknown to them I had written down her name on her papers as Marie-Noel.

There came a point where the baby was beginning to respond to the name Hadija, so I summoned up the courage and called her Marie-Noel out loud. They just stared at me like I was crazy, but I told them to call her what they wanted while I called her what I wanted to. For a while we settled on that—they called her Hadija while I called her Marie-Noel.

The secret of the official papers lasted only a little while. Aboubakar's father started to suspect I had written down a Christian name, so one day he asked me for the birth certificate of the baby. At this point I didn't know what to do, because I thought the hospital had already sent it to the registry. I had not seen the birth certificate but I knew the hospital would write what I put down. Aboubakar went and got the birth certificate and was he ever mad! He came up to me angrily and asked if I knew what it would mean if his father sees that I had written down Marie-Noel instead of Hadija. He said he was beginning to believe I was deceiving them to make them think I was with them when I really wasn't.

He looked at me and said "You never want to agree with me about anything, do you?" I replied by telling him that wasn't the case. I told him I was his wife and would do whatever he wanted, but that his dad wasn't part of our immediate family, but extended. I told him we both needed to work together. I told him all this to make him calm down because I knew that was what he wanted to hear. I needed to make him trust me so I could get back to Nigeria. So Aboubakar didn't show the certificate to his dad and lied that I had written Hadija.

Later, Aboubakar told me we needed to do some paper work so we could return to Nigeria. He said that since I didn't want to have a traditional marriage, we should go to court and do it, so I agreed. We went to court and got married and had the paperwork signed.

The next day he took the papers and went to Sandamerine where he started processing identification cards for me and the children. The process took time and the kids were growing.

At this point, if I call Moise or Marie-Noel, it angered the family, as nobody wanted to hear Christian names. I began to notice they really wanted to get rid of me, so I stopped eating their food. Whenever Aboubakar's mum gave me food, I would throw it in the pit toilet. Sometimes I would see them performing some rituals over the food, and that frightened me. That contributed the reasons I didn't want to eat their food.

There was a neighbor of ours who was from Bamileke. She noticed I wasn't happy and wasn't eating, so one day she brought me some of their native food. She told me to always let her know when I needed food. The next day I went to visit her. I was beginning to trust her and thinking about telling her what was really going on, but I also knew she was a friend to Aboubakar's mother. Sometimes I would see them gossiping in low voices. I so hoped I could trust her and confide in her. Anytime I went to her house, she gave me food which seemed very kind.

Eventually Aboubakar's father got so mad that he told me to take my children and get out of his house. He said I wasn't ready to change my name and I called my children Christian names. He blamed Aboubakar for not being able to change me to Islam or my name to an Islamic name saying, "Aboubakar I blame you for everything. I told you to change her or get rid of her." (Meaning to kill me). He did not spare his son, and told him to leave his house because he neglected his warnings.

Two days later, we moved from his parents' house to a friend of Aboubakar, who felt sorry for me. We did not have a lot of belongings, so we traveled with our bags on our heads. In the new house, my baby girl was almost 8 month old.

Later Aboubakar took us to different friend who lived alone in his father's house. This house was better than Aboubakar's father's house because it was more modern. There were two free rooms in the house. It was a great relief for me as I was free from the torture and yelling I got from Aboubakar's father.

After living there for about a month, Aboubakar's mother started visiting us. Sometimes she brought food. I liked the place because there was space for the kids to play, and at eight months Marie-Noel began walking!

Aboubakar promised to continue processing the documents that would enable us to go back to Nigeria. Months went by, and I was getting discouraged. Aboubakar was always telling me stories about the paperwork. He didn't want me to go out, even to the market. He told me how bad the people were, and how they might kill me. At this point, I started fasting and praying. "God if You set me free from this situation, I will dedicate my life to You and help women in this same situation." Being with my children every day gave me so much joy. It helped me live through all the bad things going on and the constant stress and pressure.

One day Aboubakar left the house saying he was coming right back, but he didn't return for a week. When he finally returned, I asked where he had been. He said he went to Nigeria! Since I wanted to see my people so badly, I was surprised. I asked him to prove it. He then showed me pictures he had taken with my siblings. I started crying and telling him I wanted to see them.

"Why would you want to see them? I just brought you pictures!" He said. I asked him what he had told my mum. He said he had told her I was in school.

"But I'm not in school!" I angrily insisted on seeing my family. I looked at the pictures and didn't see my sister. I asked why my sister wasn't in the picture and he said he never asked. I started to talk about going back home. Aboubakar carried the baby on his shoulder. He started to walk away, threatening to give away the child if I did not shut up. I threatened to go to the police without fear and report my situation if I was not allowed to leave this time. As I tried to hold him back and take my kid away from him, he began to beat me. I ran outside and into the streets, with my son running behind me, from one neighbor's house to another in search of a savior— someone who could tell him to stop beating me. But no neighbor was ready to help me. This went on for about an hour. We ran in and out of about 7 to 10 houses in the community. Finally, he caught up with me and beat me violently until I almost passed out. That night, the family refused to give me dinner because of "my behavior."

8   The Walking Dead & Answered Prayers

I was now all the more eager and determined to go home. I started fasting and praying. I would fast for three days, and during that time I would sing and I would pray.

Aboubakar was enraged that I was fasting and praying. He sometimes asked me why I fasted so much—was I in search of more power? He believed that fasting and praying helped to acquire spiritual powers, and my faith was stronger than his. He feared that at some point, I would be able to get away. Although I did not fully understand him, I continued to do what I knew best to do: fasting and praying.

One week after I started fasting and praying, in his dreams Aboubakar began to see his dead relatives get up from their graves and walk towards him with weapons in their hands. He started screaming and waking up at night because of the nightmares. He would wake me up to pray for him because people were after him. Every night, he was sweating and scared, pleading, asking for some prayers, saying "I can see my late uncle, aunts, friends, cousins. Please, please, pray for me! Let them go away. They are tormenting me!" I prayed earnestly until he confirmed to me that they had gone away, then I would go back to bed. After about three hours he would scream again, calling the names of his dead relatives. I would pray again. My prayers became a comfort for him because anytime I prayed the nightmares stopped.

He stopped going out because he believed his dead relatives were after him and he was terrified. He didn't want to leave my side because he didn't know when the spirits would wake up to torment him again, as it was my prayers that pushed them back. This continued every night for about a week.

The eighth day at 1:00 a.m. he began to cry out. Suddenly, he became very quiet, but still sweating and shallow breathing. Not knowing what had just taken place, I went back to sleep.

At 6:00 a.m., I woke everyone up as usual, but Aboubakar refused to wake up. He was lethargic and could not speak. I spoke to him several times. I got frightened and laid my hands on him and prayed. He was sweating profusely. I checked his temperature with the back of my hand; it was high. I watched over him for two days. The situation wasn't improving—he was getting worse. On the third day his eyes were closed and he couldn't talk or move, so I ran outside and yelled for help. Normally the young man in the house goes out and comes back home without us even knowing, so I didn't realize he was home as I yelled for help. When he heard me yell he came out to see Aboubakar. Other neighbors came too, to see what was wrong. I didn't want people to think I had done something to him!

The young man we were staying with knew something spiritual was happening. He told me he had been upset with the way we had been disturbing the house, yelling and praying at night calling the name of Jesus, disturbing his sleep.

They brought Aboubakar out of the bedroom to the living room. Neighbors who were herbalists came and prepared some concoctions and made lots of incantations to wake him up, but it obviously did not work. They started in the morning and at 2:00 p.m. it still wasn't working. They said they had tried their best and he should be taken to the hospital. Deep down in my heart I thought this could be my escape route! Even though I wanted him to wake up for the most part, I really wanted to go home.

Again I began to pray and asked that he be taken to the big hospital in town. There the doctor said he was in a coma. After 3 days, he was revived, but was told it will take him some time to be fully recovered.

I felt like I was running out of time to get free. I asked the caregivers if I could take him to Nigeria for further and proper treatment, and the doctor agreed! Here was my opportunity. God was moving on my behalf! I ran to the church, told the pastor my plans to save Aboubakar's life, and I was given 100.00 CFA Francs to help me with transportation. I prepared 3 suitcases, rented a taxi, and with the kids riding along, arrived at the hospital. I picked him up from the hospital, and we were off to the car park.

On the way from Foumbot to Foumban, Aboubakar told me, "I am not going back to Nigeria, take me back home to Foumbot." I took advantage of the fact that he was too fatigued and weak to attack me. We took another vehicle from Foumban, north to the Nigerian border. At the border, I knew it was over, and I was home! We traveled nights and days, non stop. Finally, we got home with Aboubakar still very fatigued and my baby running a high fever with congested nose.

It was midnight when the taxi finally pulled in to the house where my mother and siblings were living at Boundary Road, Benin City. My mother and neighbors came running out to welcome us. Imagine the big surprise on their faces when they saw the babies with me! They asked many questions like, "whose are they and when did you have them?" I explained to everyone that night that they were both of our kids, Aboubakar and I.

My mother and I rushed my baby to Faith Medical Center because she was dehydrated and running a fever, while Aboubakar went to see a doctor for his condition.

At this point, Aboubakar had pleaded for forgiveness and promised to marry me, pay my bride price and love me. I agreed to give it a try because of my two children. From then, I began to pretend to be happy, trying to love him so that we could become a family. I decided to keep my secrets to myself because I wanted my family to love him and accept him as my husband.

Many days passed. He received treatments and we continued to live in the one room house with my mother and siblings.

After 2 months, Aboubakar said, "We need to go back to Cameroon." I was confused, surprised, and scared, but also very determined.

I replied, "No, I will not! As a matter of fact, you were going to visit my dad, pay my bride price, get married and live as husband and wife. Moreover, I am trying to put everything behind me and start a new life with you for the sake of the children and God."

Moise and Marie-Noel

He said, "We have to go back!" I thought to myself that if he tried anything, I would go straight to the police.

My mother suggested it was time for my son to begin school. Since neither Aboubakar or I were working, I tried to talk her out of it, but she insisted. She paid to have him in kindergarten. Soon, I began to ask Aboubakar to get a job and help mother with bills and caring for the family. He started to leave the house occasionally, then daily, and then stayed a couple days away from home at a time.

One night, very late, he left again. Because I never knew where he went or where he lived and slept, I decided to follow him by hiding behind huge trees along Airport Road. He walked towards the Air force Barracks right after Ihama Junction. He walked further and turned into the Barracks and headed straight for the mosque and started to pray.

When I could not go any further, I called out to him and said, "So this is where you live now as though you have no home and family! I see you are still a Muslim. Have a good night and sleep well." He tried to follow me, yelling out that he was going to kill me and the kids. Frightened, I turned around and went home, ready to put up a fight if he followed me.

The next day, at 7:00 a.m., he showed up at the house and said, "I have told you before, we are going back to Cameroon."

I replied, "I will not go and you cannot take the kids from me again." He turned around and left. I was so relieved!

Meanwhile, I returned to my church and began to attend with my new family; just the kids and I. During the week, we walked to the church in the evenings. On Sundays, we attended Sunday school and service.

On our way to the church, I began to notice that we had some admirers, or so I thought. Once we arrived at Ihama junction and Oni street, some children were begging to see the kids and I. After a few weeks of this, I thought it was no longer some kind of admiration, so, I decided to find out what this was all about.

One Sunday morning on our way to the church, one of the young children opened their gate and called out "Abdusalam!" My son looked at them, looked at me, and looked away. Immediately, I knew that these children knew my son somehow. I thought I'd better stop by the compound find out.

After church service, I hurried out of the church because I knew it was going to be a long day. I stopped at the gate on the street of Oni and proceeded to knock. Two boys came out, saw my kids and I, and ran back into the house to call their mother. As soon as their mother set her eyes on my son, she looked surprised and happy. She invited us into her sitting room. Passionately, she carried my boy in her arms and began to speak with him. The other children seemed like they were happy to see him too. The woman asked me who I was to my son.

I replied, "He is my son and his name was never Abdusalam, but Moise. As you all already know, we are Christians and we go to the church down the street."

Quickly, she said, "Oh yes, we know this very well because we watch you pass by the street to go to church, but we did not know you had anything to do with Aboubakar."

She continued, "Aboubakar told us the baby's mother was dead in a house fire caused by the Archbishop. We were so angry and sympathized with our brother and we took the child and cared for him. I cared for him like my own son and he had brothers and sisters."

The woman never had a child of her own. She cared for and trained her nephews and nieces and so, she was happy that my son was given to her. She asked me many questions like, where do I live...am I from here...how did I know Aboubakar, and many other questions. I responded to all her questions, told her all that had transpired between me and Aboubakar.

After about an hour, we bid goodbye. I left there happy that I have been able to find out where my son was when Aboubakar took him from me, but at the same time I was sad that I did not know that he lived close to me during all that time.

I felt anguish. "Oh I could have been with my son! All that time he was right there! I could have called the cops, I could have and I should have…" I thought. It was so hard to process these thoughts. My heart ached with the pain of it all.

Life went on and we quickly settled into a routine. With the children I attended family meetings and get-togethers, especially during the Christmas season. At the family gatherings arranged by my mother's family, I often felt unwelcome. I didn't let it bother me that much because I thought, "Maybe I will be married soon and I will be accepted and respected by my family again."

Then, our peace was disturbed. One day four uniformed, armed men and one man in civilian clothes stormed our one bedroom house looking for me. Answering the door, I asked what the problem was.

The first armed man said, "We want to see Aboubakar."

I replied, "He does not live here and if I may ask, why you are looking for him?"

The second armed man replied, "We need to speak to you at the police station."

I agreed to be there the following day, right after I dropped the children at school, and the men left.

Meanwhile, my mother had found a new and affordable place for our growing family; a bungalow with a manageable roof leak. We were in the process of moving when the police asked me to come.

The next day, I dropped off my son at school and stopped by the police station with my mother and my brother, Ebenezer. I felt nervous and apprehensive.

We were directed to the office of the DPO (divisional police officer). He was a Northern Nigerian man with a strong Hausa accent. In Nigeria, people from the North are mostly Hausa tribes and their religion is Islam. The DPO was a Muslim. He quickly let us in his office and told us to feel at home, as he just wanted to ask some questions and verify some things. He asked if and how I knew Aboubakar and other questions following.

"How did you meet him? What did you do with him and what is your relationship together?" He asked.

I answered all his questions truthfully and briefly.

He went on. "At this point, we have him in custody and in chains, because he is a very bad man. My men picked him up yesterday in the mosque where he was hiding."

In my curiosity, I asked, "What did he do wrong, why is he arrested?"

The DPO explained, "He was involved in some suspicious activity, very dishonest, and appeared and disappeared whenever he wanted, especially when people started asking questions. When he was finally apprehended, he had in his possession some false and illegal documents, fake IDs and disturbing photos that we could not understand," He said.

He continued, "We came to you because someone had seen him enter your compound some days back and we thought perhaps there was someone or something here that could lead to his whereabouts."

I sat down and for the first time in the presence of my mother and brother, I began to narrate my ordeals. We all broke down in tears as the DPO and other police officers around shook their heads and felt sorry for me. The DPO was shocked that the 2 children were mine.

"Aboubakar told us, they do not belong to you, but some other woman had them and she died during the second baby's birth. You have the babies only because he put them in your custody while he is here in Nigeria. "He also said their mother had died in a fire set by the late Archbishop Idahosa before he passed away," the DPO continued. "He went further to show me a picture of a graveyard where his father held a shovel helping my son throw some soil in the hole. Are these true?" He asked

"No sir!" I quickly responded. "I am the mother to both of these children, they are mine, please believe me!" I broke down sobbing.

Then he told me to go get the children from school. "Go and get the kids, I'd like to see them. Are they both boys or girls?" He asked.

"I have a boy and a girl, sir," I responded as I turned away to take my leave. I picked up the kids from the school and returned with them to the station immediately, crying and pleading that they were indeed mine.

The DPO said, "I believe you. That man is a lunatic and you should be happy that you are alive. I don't know why he spared your life, but you should consider yourself a miracle!"

He then ordered that Aboubakar should be brought before us. In chains, hands and feet, he was led into the office looking very lean and dehydrated. He knelt down facing the DPO, speaking in Arabic.

The DPO responded, "You are not a good Muslim, I don't even think you are a Muslim or a Christian. You are an evil man. Why do you want to ruin the life of this girl?"

Aboubakar kept silent and he was led away. The DPO told me to be careful, take good care of the kids, and report to him if I have any needs and other problems. He said Aboubakar would be taken to Abuja, the nation's capital, for further trials and court processes.

They promised me that I am free and should not have anything to do with him ever again.

After six months news reached me that Aboubakar had been deported back to Cameroon never to come back to Nigeria again! Crying, I felt relieved that the children and I were COMPLETELY FREE. No one will threaten to take the kids away, coerce me or force me back to Cameroon. Neither Aboubakar nor his father will coerce or force me to convert to any religion that is against my wishes again. I am forever grateful to the Nigerian police and God for giving me back my life and helping me keep my babies..

Life almost returned to normal. Mother loved the children and cared for us all, even though she was faced with pressure from family members and co-workers to throw us out into the streets.

At this point, I was bent on going back to school. Mother paid for me to get back on track. I started to take lessons for the West African examination council (WAEC) and other classes that I needed to begin school. I began to look for jobs to help my mother pay bills and feed the children. I got teaching jobs in private schools around Benin where I taught French language.

Years passed by and the children grew. My son was now 9 years old and my daughter 7. Both were in school and doing well. To my huge relief, we never got news of Aboubakar again.

The new house, despite its crumbling condition, was a good place for us because it was large enough to accommodate us all, including my mother, and brothers. Sometimes my brothers lived with us and sometimes they went to my father's.

9 Death, Riots, Beatings

Cotonou, Benin Republic

After a time, I decided it was time for us to move away to forget all that had happened. I wanted to relocate to a place where I could make good use of my French language skills and maybe get a degree in it as well.

I relocated to Cotonou, Benin Republic (a large port city on the south coast of Benin), where we lived for about 6 months.

In Cotonou, I lived with a Pastor and family, helping with the church and working as a French interpreter at the port. Life was hard. We had to sleep on the church floor. After 6 months of this hard life, I decided to go back home to my mother.

Meanwhile, my sister Irene was living in Germany and thought that it was a good idea if I moved with her and began a new life. The idea sounded great, but "How possible could that be?" I asked myself. She had sent invitations multiple times, but the embassy kept denying visas. In my heart I never gave up.

Then tragedy hit our family again. One early morning in 2008, we woke up at 5:30 a.m. as usual. Everyone was getting ready to go about the day's business. We gathered in the living room to pray. My mother asked us, "Does anyone have a dream that they would like to share?"

"No, I do not," I replied

"Yes, I had one," said my older brother.

"In my dream, I saw many people rioting at Sapele road," he replied. "There were many armored vehicles everywhere. There were cops and people running to find shelter," he continued.

My mother prayed against rioting and war. We sang praises, read the scriptures, prayed some more, and dispersed.

In that house were two separate rooms with bathrooms and toilets. It was a big house with a big kitchen and a yard. It had two bungalows behind it where our neighbors lived. I decided to get my children ready for school and my brother's wife did the same (they had two children).

The house had run out of cooking kerosene and my brother planned to take the kids to the school on Sapele Road and proceed to the famous gas station that served the area. At the gas station, kerosene and other fuel commodities were affordable for everyone far and near. At 7:30 a.m., my brother had the kids in the car. My mother went to drop them off at school and we all bid them bye.

At 9:00, my youngest brother came driving into the yard, crying and yelling with a loud voice saying, "Brother Ebenezer is dead! Brother Ebenezer is dead!"

"Are you going crazy?" I asked him.

He said, "No, I mean it! Brother Ebenezer was shot at the gas station by an armed policeman and he is dead!"

At this time, mother was walking to the hospital to work. My brother drove, picked her up and together we went to the gas station.

We cried and cried asking God, "Lord, why?"

My brother was killed while he tried to get to the gas pump. There were many people gathered at the station wanting to get fuel and kerosene because there was a serious scarcity of petroleum products in the town and state at large. The intention was not to shoot my brother or anyone, but the cop happened to misfire. My brother was killed instantly. Immediately, the area people began to riot against the police and the police returned fire and tear gas as my brother was taken to the hospital.

Back at home, many family members and friends had gathered to comfort my mother. People cried and wailed because my brother was loved and missed.

I cried too, and asked, "God why would You let this happen to us? We have already been through so much! Why?"

In November, as burial plans were being organized, his 6 month old child was electrocuted in the house and died. Tragedy upon tragedy! Now, it was beginning to look like God had abandoned us. We continued to cry, to fast, and to pray for God to intervene and help us. Many people joined to sympathize and pray with each member of the family.

After the death of my late brother's son, he was immediately buried. The next day a pastor approached my family and asked that his body be exhumed for prayers because he believed that miracles still happened. Meanwhile, I was at home entertaining the guests who were visiting and sympathizing with us.

I had heard that the child was exhumed and I hastily went to the church where he was laid and prayed for him, wanting to see a miracle. The child was laid on the altar wrapped up in cloth. Four days after the death of the child and two days after all the prayers and fasting, the child did not have any signs of life in him, and he was reburied.

During this time, I got an invitation to do French language interpretation in Lagos State. A pastor had told me about a company that needed a French language interpreter, because they were going to hold an international convention. They told me to negotiate my amount of pay. I called the company and we settled for 100,000 Naira including my flight ticket.

Two days before I flew to Lagos, my mother gave me a call saying, "I need you to come to Sapele Road, at your father's house. There is a family meeting going on and the family needs your presence."

I said, "Mother, I don't think it is a good idea for me to show up because I am scared that my family does not like me."

My extended family did not like me because I was not married and I have two children that have no father and were born out of wedlock. So I had every reason to be scared. My maternal family was the most scary because they were viciously wicked. My mother assured me that it was going to be fine.

Immediately, I called for a motorbike, hopped on it and rode to my father's house at Sapele road. I got there and right outside the house were many family members—maternal and paternal extended members.

As I approached them, I bowed my knee to greet every one of them as culture demands. Sitting there were my father, uncles, aunties, and even others that I know. One of my uncles from my maternal family asked me to get on my knees. I asked why but he yelled at me to kneel down. I obeyed quickly. One of my aunts came closer and gave me a slap on the face. At this point, I began to cry.

"What have I done?" I asked apologetically and afraid.

'Shut up! Using both of your hands, cover your mouth, now!" replied my aunt.

I tried to escape but it was too late. I was surrounded by all of them, my mother sitting helplessly in a corner looking sad and fearful. Finally, they decided to tell me what I had allegedly done.

My younger uncle proceeded to say, "The allegations brought against you are that you have refused to go to school when your father paid for you to get educated. You went to Cameroon and came back with 2 children, unmarried, and they have a non-native as their father. You ordered your nephew to be exhumed for prayers because you believed he was going to be revived, which is an abomination according in our culture."

"No, these allegations are not true!" I exclaimed. "Father never cared for me, he drove me away with my mother because of Christianity. I did not order my nephew to be exhumed. I didn't run away to have children in Cameroon, I can explain." I continued as I began to cry in terror.

"You beat up your father's wife!" my uncle continued.

"That is not true at all, I don't even fight," I continued to defend myself even though they would not listen to my side of the story. They were just hungry to beat me.

Another of my mother's brothers' stood up in the gathering. "I know you all are angry against her, but I guarantee you that this girl was not present during the exhumation of the dead baby. That I assure you. She was busy with her travel issues."

"We have not asked you any questions here, we do not need anyone's input at this time. Please be seated," replied my younger uncle. My older uncle tried to save me, but other family members did not agree with him, so he stopped.

My younger uncle asked my brother to go get him some canes. The canes were made of birch wood and are used to flog the backsides, bare legs, or across the hands. Before I showed up, they had planned it all and hid the four canes away from all eyes. As soon as the signal was given, the canes were brought out.

My uncle commanded me, "Lay down flat on your belly."

"Please uncle, I have done nothing wrong, forgive me, don't beat me" I pleaded.

"You are no good, lay down flat or I will flog you all over your body!"

"Uncle, I have my menstrual period right now. Please have mercy on me," I continued to plead for my life.

"Stretch her out," beckoning on others, he yelled out as he ordered them.

Four heavy men came to me, grabbed me and stretched me out. The first one was holding my left hand, the second one holding my right hand, the third held my left leg, and the forth one, the right leg. It was the time of the month that I was on my period. Wearing a skirt did not hide my period from the onlookers and  passers-by since this was taking place outside of the house. As the canes landed on my back, all four at the same time, I screamed and screamed. My uncle got tired and another decided to help him out. He took another four and joined in the flogging. So, two of them flogged and flogged as I struggled to get free. I could not turn to face any other direction since I was held strongly by these heavy men. I cried for help and I began to cry for death to take me. I was flogged until the canes began to break and tear apart. It continued until I could no longer cry. I cried until I did not feel pain anymore.

Suddenly, as I stopped crying, even though the beating continued, I stopped struggling. There was a point at which the flogging stopped because they thought I was dead. The canes were all broken and torn. They let me fall to the ground, turned me around, and hit me with their shoes when they found that I was still breathing. Then, they told me to kneel down again and I did, shaking all over.

The meeting ended and everyone left for their various homes. I could see some of them sympathizing with me, but they could not help me. Arriving home to my mother's compound that evening with my red and swollen eyes and marks of canes all over my body, bleeding, I hated my family members, paternal and maternal. I thought, "I do not belong to this family." I just wanted to go far away and never return. I wanted a place of love and harmony, or at least a place I could never be beaten again. I wanted to go away with my children to a place I could become a nurse.

10 God's Timing, God's Healing

In January of 2009, my sister sent me an invitation to Germany. This time, we decided to travel without the children and come back for them later in order to facilitate migration. This time, I had to travel with my mother.

My mother, with all these tragedies, needed some place to go away and relax. We went to the embassy and this time victory! We were called to come get our passports with visas to Germany in them. We traveled again to Lagos, collected our passports with our visas and bought tickets.

In March of 2009, we set off to Lagos state to get on the plane. I opened the gate to leave and said goodbye to my children.

"When are you coming back?" My son asked.

"I don't know, but I promise to come back soon," I answered, as I began to cry, not knowing when I would see them again or when we would be reunited.

Before leaving for Germany.

Although flying on the airplane was an amazing experience, I could not stop thinking and praying for my children for God to keep them from my angry and fierce family.

We left Nigeria at almost midnight and arrived in Germany at 6:30 in the morning. My sister was waiting to pick us up. I had not seen my sister for close to 11 years. As soon as we picked up our bags and luggage, we met my sister and she drove us to Baumholder, Germany.

On our way, I saw the snow for the first time in my life. "It is beautiful out here." I thought to myself. I thought I was already in heaven because I have always envisioned heaven to be as white as snow. I was excited, but my excitement only lasted for a few minutes as I thought of my children. I missed them already. I wanted them to be safe.

My sister was happily married and living on the military base. I thought it was beautiful and I wanted to live there and never go back to Nigeria.

I immediately started classes to obtain a general education development (GED). I obtained my GED in December of 2009, obtained my diploma in 2010.

Baumholder, Germany

After 6 months in Germany, news reached me that my father had passed away. I remembered being angry and at the same time sorrowful and was deciding if I wanted to be part of his burial.

One Saturday morning, one of my half brothers called me on the phone and said, "I encourage you to be part of our father's burial."

"Why,?" I asked.

"Because he is still our father, no matter what he has done to anyone. We have to forgive him, so send in your contribution for the burial ceremony. Are you coming to the burial ceremony?" he asked me.

"No," I replied.

I could not return to Nigeria to be part of the ceremony because I got a visa to go with my sister and husband to the United States of America. I had to travel from Germany to America the same time as the burial, so I could not return home to attend.

On September 10th 2010, I flew to the United States of America, the country of freedom and hope. The flight to New York was a smooth one, but from New York to Hartford, Connecticut was rough because of the weather.

Overall, I had hope that this was true freedom. Meanwhile, I continued to miss my children very much. At times I could hardly bear it. Two months after my arrival in Connecticut, I got a job at the Foxwoods Casino as a cashier. Because that job paid the minimum wage of $9.00, I decided to find another job where I could save some money to go to school and bring my children to live with me. I found another cashier job at a Lowe's store. This one paid $12.00 an hour.

After about 6 months, I started working on my nursing career. I took a certified nursing assistant (CNA) class for 2 weeks and wrote my exam. After obtaining my certification, I applied for so many jobs via the internet, including a phlebotomist with the American Red Cross.

By now, my sister lived in New York. One weekend, I traveled to visit her, and 2 days later I received a phone call from the American Red Cross to come in for an interview for the position of a phlebotomist! Immediately, I returned to Connecticut, attended the interview, got the job, and started training right away.

I enjoyed working as a phlebotomist because I had to travel to draw blood. There were a lot of interactions with people from all walks of life. In particular, the screening questions were very interesting.

The drive to become a nurse consumed me. I enrolled part time at Three Rivers Community College in Norwich to take prerequisites into the nursing program, attending classes in the evenings and weekends. I enjoyed school and so I continued.

Meanwhile, I decided to file for immigration status for my kids to have them get visas and join me in the U.S. This process took me about another 2 years because I only had a green card, which is the alien registration status.

Becoming a U.S. citizen was the best thing I ever decided at that time. All the while, I did not miss a day of buying calling cards and talking on the phone with my children because I wanted to stay close to their hearts.

After one year of working, I decided to move to another state. At this time, my sister had traveled back to Germany and I felt lonely.

Finally in September of 2013, my children's' visas to the United States were approved! In November of that same year, I had enough money to fly to Nigeria and be reunited with them. My joy was full again! I had missed them and I wanted to see them grow. We were together again!

In December of that same year, the children and I moved from Connecticut to Michigan. I immediately registered for classes at Grand Rapids Community College (GRCC). When I was told that the registered nursing (RN) program had a wait list of 3-1/2 to 5 years, I decided to get on the practical nurse (LPN) wait list which was just about a year. I started with my prerequisite classes for the LPN program while I worked here and there.

In 2015, my journey to become a nurse began. The LPN program was only a year, and I was done in December of 2016. I thought that was it, but I was not satisfied with being just an LPN. It was just the beginning of my nursing journey. I went ahead for the RN program.

I attended Montcalm Community College and got my license in 2019.

I still had a strong desire to help people, and thought of my homeland often. But within me, I tried to struggle to make that desire go away so that I would forget about Nigeria and Africa for good.

"Life in the United States is beautiful, free from all the problems that I encountered in my homeland," I thought to myself.

Patience Karsten, BSN, RN

Patience Karsten, RN

I loved being here, I loved the feeling of freedom, but my feelings from my past never went away. I began to struggle with trusting, forgiveness, and relationship issues—carrying these along not only in my heart, but in my flesh and bones every minute of the day.

Remembering the day I was raped, the feeling and pain stuck in my head, messing with issues of trust and sexuality. The pain from the beatings stuck in my flesh and bones eating me up like a cankerworm. Reliving every moment of it hurts, even to this day. I felt really uncomfortable whenever I remembered my past. I reflected always and cried severely and bitterly every time I remembered my beatings and my past hurts, both mental and physical.

I knew my experiences were part of me. They followed me everywhere I went, and at times I felt like I was reliving it. Flashes of these experiences burst into my mind every time some ongoing life issues or activities remind me of it, staring into my face like a masquerade. It felt like it was right there waiting to get a hold of me and choke me. I felt it, lived it, saw it, and bore it all over again. The hatred, the shame, and the discomfort it created in me weighed on me like a burden. The weight was heavy, the unforgiveness was real, and the visible scars left behind—like the ones on my thighs from the caning—reminded me of the cruelty.

All these gradually ate me up. I knew something was not right. I knew I needed some healing. Thinking about the endless beatings in the hands of my classmates and family members from childhood to the age of 31 tortured me. I felt that my family was insensitive and barbaric. Additionally, the fact that I wore a female pad under my skirt during the caning did not stop them from holding my hands and legs exposing my female parts. They did not give me a chance to tell them what I went through. They didn't care.

At this point, I concluded that I did not have a family because they hated me and I could not figure the reason behind the hatred.

More so, my experience with Aboubakar set my heart ablaze against him, his family, and his religion.

Finally, I blamed God for putting me into my family, blamed myself for not listening to God's direction, and for going to Cameroon.

One Sunday morning, at the Grand Rapids First Church (where I attended services and became a member of the deaf and hard of hearing ministry), I heard the pastor preaching forgiveness. It hit me so hard that I began to struggle within myself because I did not want to let go of unforgiveness.

I said, "How can I, it is too much, too many people wronged me!" I closed my eyes only to see the stripes of Jesus on the cross. I cried and sobbed bitterly. During this moment, I felt like something I was holding on to was about to leave me, but the pain of the separation made me cry the more. I felt like I had held on to something which was becoming really tangible, so dear to me, and it was inseparable from me. The pain of letting it go hurt so much that I screamed and screamed.

The pastor made an altar call. As I was crying, I stepped out and found myself standing in front of the altar, face to face with an associate pastor and his wife trying to calm me down. I was able to narrate a little of what was hurting me and my reasons for not wanting to forgive and let go.

"You need to forgive and be healed from this pain and unforgiveness. How long will you continue to hold on?" the associate pastor's wife asked.

This went on for about an hour until finally, I felt the struggle within me stop. I suddenly felt so free and peaceful. I was able to control my crying and I wiped my tears. They both prayed for me and I left.

From that day on, I was able to live as though nothing had happened! I even attended family reunions and participated in family matters in Nigeria.

My increasing desire to help others motivated me to begin a master's program in Family Nurse Practitioner (MSN-FNP) at Chamberlain University with an expected graduation date in 2021.

My desire has also led to the birth of two organizations: One to rescue females who are going through difficult situations and do not know where to go and get rescue. No female child should ever have to go through what I went through! For this cause, the Potters Hill Foundation has been created to rescue and equip victims of sexual exploitation and maltreatment. The second is Missionary Medics. More information on this ministry can be found on page 102.

After my mother retired from working at the Central Hospital, she was invited to the United States to spend some time away from home. After some years, she obtained a Resident Permit to live there. Today, my mother lives with my sister and I here in the United States. Although my big brother passed away, he still lives in my heart and will ever be remembered. My children live with me and they are in school. The USA is my home and I am proud to be a United States citizen.

Because I know that I will no longer experience the cruelty back home, I often thank God for getting me here. I am free and I feel free and I live free in the land of the free.

Who is Patience (Aisien) Karsten?

The following is what many say about Patience. Among them are coworkers, college professors, personal acquaintances, family and friends.

"As Patience's former university professor, Patience was relentless in her pursuit of learning and understanding. She gave her all to her coursework and graciously shared her unique life experiences and world view, steeped in her native Nigeria, with her professor and with her classmates who she lavishly enriched. Patience went above and beyond in her history course research and outshone every one of her peers in the quality and quantity of her academic submissions. Remarkable, too, was her faithful attendance at all weekly Webex live sessions, where she encouraged and inspired attendees and her professor, alike, with her genuine and boundless interest in United States history subject matter. Had this been permissible, she would have been the consummate teaching assistant. As a person, Patience's beloved Christian religion is exemplified or manifested in so much of what she does and who she truly is. Despite the unspeakable family hardships she endured in Benin, Nigeria and in Cameroon, West Africa, she has chosen to forgive her transgressors and pray and work for their redemption. The story she shares is designed to bring light and healing to others who, as trafficked victims, may find hope and a way forward to wholesome, meaningful and fulfilling lives."

Professor King, Chamberlain University, USA

"Patience Karsten is a smart, diligent, and hardworking, friendly, and brilliant lady with excellent communication skills. For over 4 years that I have known her, our interactions over the years speaks volumes of her great personality. She is caring, easy-going, witty, ambitious, resilient, and a goal getter. A devout Christian and devoted mother. She is a strategic and transformational leader, and philanthropist extraordinaire. She runs a foundation that gives back to her roots in Nigeria."
Anonymous

"Patience and I met in our first year of nursing school. We soon went our separate ways, not knowing that one day we would reconnect, not only professionally, but in our sisterhood as well. Patience got hired at our job, a place that I had been for many years. To that facility, she brought a strong love for nursing, a wealth of knowledge and a drive for success. I am always overwhelmed with joy to hear the stories of how she gives back to her community. I thank God for who she is, and for her loving, caring, servant's heart."
Gertrude Coger, LPN

Thank You!

I want to thank everyone for encouraging me to write my story, and for your support—especially Emmanuel Evbuomwan, my co-workers and Professor King.

And of course I thank God, for making a way when there seemed to be no way!

About the Author

Patience (Aisien) Karsten is a Nigerian-American author, living in Michigan, USA with her family. She is a philanthropist, volunteer, speaker, and CEO of Missionary Medics, a health awareness mission group promoting health and preventing illness in Nigeria and beyond. As a registered nurse, Patience is currently working and continues to pursue a Graduate degree in family nurse practitioner (MSN-FNP) program at Chamberlain University.

You can find more information about the ministry of Missionary Medics on page 102.

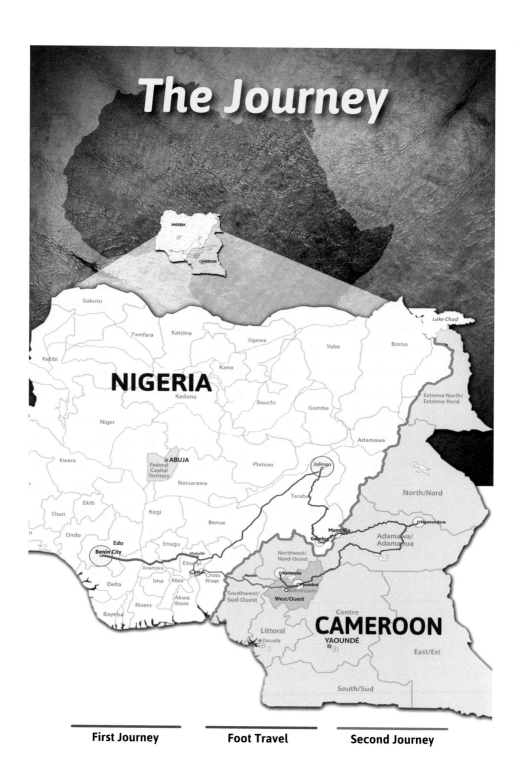

The Journey

First Journey   Foot Travel   Second Journey

Resources

Do you need to/want to know Jesus as your LORD and have questions about God, life, suffering, just depressed, or just want to chat with someone who cares? Go to the website: www.peacewithgod.net

A simple prayer:

"Dear God, I know I'm a sinner, and I ask for your forgiveness. I believe Jesus Christ is Your Son. I believe that He died for my sin and that you raised Him to life. I want to trust Him as my Savior and follow Him as Lord, from this day forward. Guide my life and help me to do your will. I pray this in the name of Jesus. Amen."

If you sincerely prayed this prayer from your heart you are now a new creation and your old life has passed away. Being born again isn't about "fire insurance" or finding religion. Being born again is a 24/7 relationship with God our Father because of the finished work of Jesus Christ—born of a virgin, lived a sinless life, was crucified (laying His life down for us sinners so we may know God as Father, and become a part of the Kingdom of God as God Himself intended from the beginning). Being a daughter/son of God is a relationship, not a denomination or religion. We recommend studying the Word of God daily to know His Word which is His will.

Need a Bible?

If you don't have a Bible and cannot afford one, you can easily access one for free on the web. There are written and audio forms of the Bible, as well as videos to help you in the best way for your unique style. One website of many is: www.biblegateway.com

What About Church?

We recommend finding a Bible-based place of worship to grow In Christ and become a part of the Body of Christ. Many local churches have websites with service times, activities, and special ministries.

Missionary Medics

A great part of my own personal healing has come by giving back to others who are hurting. As a nurse, I want to be able to help people, both here is the USA and in Africa.

Our vision for Missionary Medics is to serve as an international voice for serious health issues such as Malaria, Diabetes, COVID, AIDS, and impart health and wellness practices.

We also serve as an international voice for women and girls, teaching good health, well being, quality education and gender equality. The world is home to more than 1.1 billion girls under age 18, who are poised to become the largest generation of female leaders, entrepreneurs and change-makers the world has ever seen. Our dream is to see girls live free from gender-based violence, harmful practices, and HIV and AIDS, and to learn new skills towards the futures they choose, as they lead as a generation of activists accelerating social change.

We emphasize training and care in a way that it imparts the skills and knowledge that will remain with the community long after the team is moved on.

Learn more at www.MissionaryMedics.org
or on Facebook: www.facebook.com/missionary.medics.9
Email: missionarymedics1@gmail.com

Other Helpful Ministries in the USA:

Get Help | The National Domestic Violence Hotline

At the National Domestic Violence Hotline, advocates are available 24/7 to talk confidentially with anyone in the United States who is abused or affected by a loved one who is abused. This site has great resources: www.thehotline.org/help/

Women At Risk, International (WAR Int'l)

WAR is established to create circles of protection around those at risk for abuse, trafficking, exploitation, and more, worldwide. *"Through culturally sensitive, value-added intervention projects and partnerships, we provide safe places to heal. Our passion is to empower survivors to live and work with dignity and hope. Our programs reach over 40 countries, including the United States. Each month, additional projects and partnerships are formed, increasing our ability to offer the rescued and at-risk a hand-up instead of a handout."*
https://warinternational.org/

Are you struggling with deep hurts in your life? Or habits you just can't break free of? Celebrate Recovery is a Christ-centered, 12 step recovery program for anyone struggling with hurts, abuse or addiction of any kind. CR is a safe place to find community and freedom from the issues that are affecting our lives. Many churches have active CR groups, which are also listed by city on their website:
www.celebraterecovery.com

Suicide Prevention

The National Suicide Prevention Lifeline is a national network of local crisis centers that provides free, confidential emotional support to people in suicidal crisis or emotional distress 24 hours a day, 7 days a week. **Call 1-800-273-8255** or go to the website for a private, live chat:
https://suicidepreventionlifeline.org/

Struggling with the aftermath of an abortion?

Pat Layton is Founder and President of **Surrendering the Secret**, a post-abortion recovery ministry focused on healing heartbreak after abortion: www.surrenderingthesecret.com

---

Book Design

Patience created this book together with her friend, artist, designer and photographer **Lynn Hitchcock**. Lynn is the owner of Inspired Graphics, a graphic design firm located near Grand Rapids, MI. You can see more examples of her work at www.InspiredGraphics.org

---

Has "Never Give Up" touched your life? Need help overcoming trauma or know someone who does?

This is for you! Patience's NEW book is coming out soon! *Overcoming Trauma,* outlines steps to freedom from the effects trauma and abuse.